LETTERS TO
A YOUNG
MUSLIM

LETTERS TO A YOUNG MUSLIM

OMAR SAIF GHOBASH

PICADOR

NEW YORK

www.picadorusa.com • picadorbookroom.tumblr.com
www.twitter.com/picadorusa • www.facebook.com/picadorusa

Picador® is a U.S. registered trademark and is used by Macmillan
Publishing Group, LLC, under license from Pan Books Limited.

For book club information, please visit www.facebook.com
/picadorbookclub or e-mail marketing@picadorusa.com.

Designed by Jonathan Bennett

Library of Congress Cataloging-in-Publication Data

Names: Ghobash, Omar Saif, 1971– author.
Title: Letters to a young Muslim / Omar Saif Ghobash.
Description: New York : Picador, 2017.
Identifiers: LCCN 2016039168 (print) | LCCN 2016041725 (e-book) |
    ISBN 9781250119841 (hardcover) | ISBN 9781250119834 (e-book)
Subjects: LCSH: Islam—21st century. | Muslim youth. | Islamic
    sociology. | Ghobash, Omar Saif, 1971– | Ambassadors—United
    Arab Emirates—Biography. | BISAC: RELIGION / Islam /
    General. | RELIGION / Islam / Theology. | SOCIAL SCIENCE /
    Customs & Traditions. | SOCIAL SCIENCE / Islamic Studies.
Classification: LCC BP161.3 .G563 2017 (print) | LCC BP161.3 (e-book) |
    DDC 297.09/051—dc23
LC record available at https://lccn.loc.gov/2016039168

Our books may be purchased in bulk for promotional, educational, or
business use. Please contact your local bookseller or the Macmillan
Corporate and Premium Sales Department at 1-800-221-7945, extension
5442, or by e-mail at MacmillanSpecialMarkets@macmillan.com.

First Edition: January 2017

10 9 8 7 6 5 4 3 2 1

To my mother for all her patience, generosity, and sacrifice.
And I promise my Abdullah a novel.

CONTENTS

Author's Note ix

Preface xi

The Questions You Face 1

The Gray Area 7

Landscapes of Islam 25

Wealth, Opportunity, and Repentance 37

Fragments of Memory 45

The Limits of What We Can Know 53

My First Dark Days 57

Who on Earth Told You That? 69

What Is True Islam? 75

"Islam Is a Religion of Peace" 79

Crisis of Authority 85

Responsibility 89

The Perspective of an Outsider 105

Path to Fundamentalism 119

Violence 131

Role Models 139

The Challenge of Freedom 151

Our Complex Entanglement with the West 159

Revelation and Reason 165

Sermons and What to Expect in the Mosque
  on Fridays 175

Good Deeds and Bad Deeds 183

The Quran and the Search for Knowledge 187

How We Construct Ourselves and the Past 197

Men and Women 209

Free Speech and the Silence Within Ourselves 219

A Closer Look at a Moral Conundrum 229

The Muslim Individual 237

Acknowledgments 245

AUTHOR'S NOTE

Out of respect for the Prophet Mohammed, it is customary to say the words "peace be upon him" or a variant of this phrase whenever he is mentioned. In print this is abbreviated to PBUH. Here, in the letters, I assume the reader utters it as appropriate.

PREFACE

I have two sons. My older son, Saif, was born in 2000 and my younger son, Abdullah, in 2004. Their presence in my life has provided me a framework for living. If I thought I had purpose as a bachelor, I discovered much greater purpose and meaning through my children, and with my wife. Whereas life as a bachelor meant looking out for myself, starting a family brought a sense of balance and responsibility that I could not have imagined. The responsibilities that come with building a family enable you to take a step back from yourself and see that the world consists of other people with greater claims on your energy and time than you yourself. Their existence provides the ground for my actions in the world. I feel an infinite obligation toward my children, who are still dependent on me and their mother for guidance and protection. I used to think that ideas and attitudes were something of interest but of no great importance. Matters would resolve themselves, things would work out. Now that I have children, I see the world through a broader lens. Now what happens in the world matters very much. And whose ideas dominate matters. In coming to this realization, I also recognized that the obligation of care and protection that I owe my children extends further. It extends more generally toward those of us who do not have the means to control their lives or who depend on others for the structure of our communities and societies.

I am the ambassador of the United Arab Emirates to Russia. The United Arab Emirates is located on the tip of the Arabian Peninsula, just south of Iran and east of Saudi Arabia. Our population was traditionally a mix of desert dwellers and seafaring pearl divers and goods traders. Today, we have a population approaching ten million, with over 180 nationalities represented. People live, work, and worship in peace alongside one another. I have been ambassador from January 2009 until today. I have had the privilege to be an observer of international relations from at least three very different perspectives. Because I speak English, Arabic, Russian, and French, and have friends and colleagues in the United States, Europe, Russia, and the Arab world, I have had access to the thinking that takes place within different cultures and political systems. The longer I perform my job, the more I am convinced of the power of ideas, and language, to move the world to a better place.

The world I grew up in was one where ideas floated around but had little connection with reality. I would hear about dreams of a new world order based on a very straightforward type of Islam. We were taught to pray and how to read the Quran. We were always told that certain actions were haram. *Haram* and *halal* are terms used to describe things that are prohibited (haram) or allowed (halal). Strangely though, most of the time we were told things were haram—not allowed. Eating pork and drinking alcohol seemed to fill people with horror. These were definitely haram. What else was haram? Lying and stealing—or taking things that were not yours—were haram. Hurting others or yourself were also haram—since the body and life are gifts from Allah. Suicide in particular would send you straight to the fiery Hereafter, since this was taking what did not belong to you but rather to Allah. We were taken to the mosque on Fridays for the communal midday prayer. The sermons would be shouted out and people would stare into space until it was time for the short prayer. It was a pleasant feeling. You were surrounded by all types of people from laborers to millionaires. All lined up in orderly rows praying the same prayers and shaking hands with one another at the end of the ceremony.

Then there was what I would call fundamentalist

Islam. What did this mean? It meant that the world would go back to what it was like at the height of the Islamic Empires of the seventh and eighth centuries. These ideas were repeated in school and after. The ideas always contrasted strongly with the world that surrounded us. This was a sense of their weakness in the world and their destruction at the hands of others. This was the time of the Lebanese civil war that began in 1975, and then the Iran–Iraq war, which lasted from 1980 to 1988. The return to the practices of our seventh- and eighth-century Muslim forefathers we were promised would bring us back the power, the glory, and the success that they enjoyed. There was another layer to the things we were taught. It did not always surface, but it was always there, I realize now. It was all the ideas that seemed to contradict earlier lessons. Ideas like suicide bombing. People would say that it was a great sacrifice to give your life for the community or the country or the Islamic Ummah, the global community of Muslims. My friends and I would ask how it was possible that committing suicide was seen as a great sin against Allah if done for reasons such as sadness, or unhappiness; and yet it was the greatest sacrifice a Muslim could make if it was done to fight the "enemy"? This question was relevant in the 1980s when I was a teenager, and is still relevant today.

Words in the air, until September 11, 2001. When the

Twin Towers in New York were destroyed in the most shocking terrorist incident of my lifetime, I realized those words had now become a reality. The words that I had listened to and absorbed when I was a child had now taken on meaning in the world around me. These words were now creating a reality with consequences not just for Americans and Europeans but also for me and my fellow Muslims in the Arab world.

My first son was born in December 2000. I remember carrying him in a child sling on my chest in the summer of 2001—as we visited Manhattan. A few days after we got back to Dubai, we witnessed the terrible events of 9/11 on CNN. I felt an overwhelming sense of responsibility toward this child. I decided that the time had come for me to take action in the limited ways that I could. I involved myself in the arts, in literature and education. My overwhelming desire was to open up areas of thought, language, and imagination in order to show myself and my fellow Muslims that our world has so much more to offer us than the limited fantasies of deeply unhappy people.

My work in diplomacy came later, and I have approached it with the same attitude of openness to ideas and possibilities. Through travel and interaction with all kinds of people, from the deeply religious to the highly knowledgeable, from the deeply uneducated to the hyperconnected, I see the common humanity that we all share. When I hear of different value systems and how they are going to clash, I see the values of human beings striving for a better life. I write these letters to both of my sons, and to all young Muslim men and women, with the intention of opening their eyes to some of the questions they are likely to face and the range of possible answers that exist for them. I want to show them that there are questions that have persisted from the first beginnings of human thought, and that there is no reason for the modern Muslim not to engage with them as generations before them did. I want to reaffirm the duty to think and question and engage constructively with the world. I want my sons and their generation of Muslims to understand that we live in a world full of difference and diversity.

I want them to understand how to be faithful to their inherited religion of Islam and its deepest values, as well as to see how to chart their way through a complex world. I want them to discover through observation and thought that there need be no conflict between Islam and the rest of the world. I want them to understand that even in matters of religion, there are many choices that we need to make. Not all that is presented as part and parcel of religion is necessarily the case. Much is presented as divine instruction but in fact reflects choices that other people have made for us. As I say in one of the following letters, there are structural principles in Islam, such as the search for knowledge and the command to use one's mind and think about the world around us. I want my sons' generation of Muslims to realize that they have the right to think and decide what is right and what is wrong, what is Islamic and what is peripheral to the faith. It is their burden to bear whatever decision they make.

LETTERS TO
A YOUNG
MUSLIM

THE QUESTIONS YOU FACE

Habeebie Saif,

You often ask me why I am writing a book and what it is about. Sometimes I tell you that I am writing it for you, sometimes for young Muslims like you. I watch you as you grow and I think of the challenges you have faced and will face. Sometimes I know that I am writing this set of letters for myself.

I remember when you realized that you were a Muslim. You were tiny. You were sweet and round and friendly. It was at an event at school. Your schools so far have been English-language curriculum schools and the student body came from more than a hundred nationalities. One day the students had to identify their religion and you came back "aware" of your religious identity. You took this identity very seriously. You began to ask me what you "had to do" to be a Muslim. I explained as best as I could the simple steps of knowing that the big Guy in the sky, who created the world, was really called Allah, and that hundreds of years ago, he had sent us his Messenger Mohammed with the Quran. I told you that we prayed five times a day and I reminded you of Ramadan, when we would not eat all day until the evening. Soon you were coming back from school telling me what I had to do to be a "good Muslim." It seems your Arabic teacher and his colleague, your religious studies teacher, had a better idea of what being a Muslim meant. You became a little aggressive and I began to realize that your mother and I were not the only ones bringing you up. I saw that we had competition for your attention. I panicked a little. I had images of you running away to Syria to fight in a war where people would exploit your good nature. I imagined you cutting yourself off from us, your family, because we were not strict enough Muslims according to the standards that you had picked up from these so-called teachers of yours. I had the urge to go to your school and punch them and tell them they had no right to teach you these things. Instead, I spoke to your mother repeatedly and at length. She is seven years younger than me and grew up three streets away from where I lived with my siblings. Unlike me, both her parents are from the same town in the Emirates—Al Ain. Her upbringing was more uniformly Arab and Muslim than mine could have been, given that my mother is Russian and descended from Orthodox clergymen. Your mother had also been through similar experiences. I know because we had gone to the same school. It was not that we were taught to hate groups of people in a formal way. It was the offhand comments that a teacher would make, or the playground gossip about the Jews or the Shia sect of Islam. The assumption was that you could condemn people you had never met, and who had themselves never done anything wrong. Your mother was, and is, adamant, as am I, that we are not going to let our children be educated to hate.

One by one, we spoke to you about the people you were "meant to hate." There was no reason to hate anyone. There is no reason to react to the world around you with hatred. You have to understand that someone has made the choice for you when they say you have to hate. The choice is yours and the only way you can make the world a better place is by doing the opposite of hating. It is by loving. It was not easy to change your mind. Your teachers had done a good job. This made us more determined than ever to win you back. Eventually, you came back to us and decided that hatred was unnecessary and unfair. In fact, hatred is many more things.

Recently, I celebrated my forty-third birthday. I had been waiting for this particular birthday for a long time.

From the age of nineteen. Both years were of immense importance to me as I grew up and matured. As you know, your grandfather Saif, my father, was killed in a terrorist attack in 1977. My father was forty-three when he died. When I was your age, I used to think that forty-three was a big number. Now that I have passed forty-three, I feel that life is only just beginning for me. Before I go on, let me tell you why nineteen was also such an important birthday for me. When I was twelve I discovered that the man who killed my father was nineteen when he did what he did. Nineteen. When I was twelve I asked myself whether I would be able to kill a man when I turned nineteen. I waited for the day and then I asked myself the question. The answer was no. No way. Not in a million years could I lift a gun or a rifle and shoot another man. I felt like I was still a twelve-year-old.

I looked forward to the age of forty-three and I knew I would ask myself whether I could imagine my life ending at forty-three. When my birthday came, I felt the horror of having barely scratched life. I remember thinking how little time I had spent with you. I thought back to my father and imagined the horror he must have felt as he realized that his life was slipping away from him. My siblings and I, your uncles and aunt, were all under the age of ten when your grandfather died. I look at you and I know how much more time I spend with you because of this fear, and even this is not enough.

I am writing this book for you because I want you to have a piece of paper that will be there long after I am gone. I want to give you some of the love and guidance that I wish my father had been able to give me when I was your age and older. I am writing this set of letters to you because I want you to have some idea of the questions that you will face, and some of the answers that are out there. I do not want you to hear it from others. I do not want you to learn the most important lessons in life from people who do not love you as I love you. I want you to hear the lessons from the person who loves you most. If you think that I worry too much about you, know that I worry only about you.

I want you to know about the things I believe after more than thirty years of thinking about my father's death. His death forced me to try to answer a bunch of difficult questions; it shaped the way in which I view the world.

In these letters, I will tell you how I saw the world around me when I was younger, when I was your age and when I was a little older, and how I see similar things happening to you. I want you to know that the questions you face, and the solutions you find, or are presented with, are solutions that many of us were faced with as well.

THE GRAY AREA

Habeebie Saif,

You are growing up in a world that is radically different from the world of the 1970s and 1980s in which I grew up, even though I am only twenty years or so older than you. In today's world, you have access to all the information you could want about the most obscure ideas, events, and movements. You, and I, are overwhelmed by the media coverage of Islam and Muslims, intertwined with the constant linkage with terrorism and religiously inspired violence. You find that it is difficult to be a Muslim and live in societies that seem to be made up of lonely, sullen, and isolated individuals.

Where is the meaning and purpose in all of this? When you think about the history that you are a part of, the history of a young religion with a blessed Prophet named Mohammed, who set the world on fire with the divine revelation that he carried, it is difficult to accept the mundanity of the world you live in. Of course, there are the technological wonders that appear almost daily. These technologies intrigue and entertain, they satisfy and they fill your day with activity—but they have also taken over your time even as they are meant to be of service to you. The technologies that surround us seem to free us, but there is the niggling doubt that they have enslaved us by appealing to our wildest personal whims. There is the empty electrical buzz that we are left with after a day online, checking posts, looking for information, and then being sidetracked by interesting articles. You might compensate by looking at some of the Muslim websites. You watch, you listen, you read, you absorb. The West offers temptations, both physical and moral temptations. Freedom is worshipped and the body is yours to use as you wish. The Islamic scholars online, the ulema, "those who have knowledge," have a vision of a world where Islam and the Muslims are the center. Where the Muslims set the agenda, deploy power, develop technologies, decide outcomes. The ulema online have a plan for how this is all going to happen.

You are told that it is inherent within our religion to be the dominant player. All the rules that we know about are written for an Islamic society that dominates others or at least confidently holds them at bay, at arm's length. We will give you peace if you are peaceful, otherwise, beware. Islam was dominant from the time the Prophet Mohammed converted the people of Mecca to Islam till an Islamic empire was established from the Atlantic Ocean all the way to Central Asia. Why should this not be the case again? Of today's global population of 7 billion people, 1.7 billion are Muslim. Many studies tell us that Islam is a young religion and is growing and spreading faster than any other religion.

Certain dominant strains of Islam demand that it be placed at the center of world politics. And supposedly you are obliged to be its servant. Why? Well, because we have a series of well-funded and persuasive voices who tell us daily that Islam is under attack and that we need to be on the offensive. Is this really the case? I do not believe so. These are shrill voices that have a warped view of the world and have managed to acquire finances and credibility.

They tell you that the only way Islam is going to take this dominant and deciding position is when Muslims are proper Muslims. This idea is also very simple. You are told that you are not observant enough, and only when you are observant to the correct degree, as well as those who surround you, will Islam flourish and prosper. It is your fault that Islam is in this degraded and miserable state. You are shown YouTube videos of courageous Afghan mujahideen fighting the might of the Soviet army in the 1980s. You are shown clearer videos of the war in Bosnia of the 1990s. More recent and more shocking videos come from the aftermath of the U.S. invasion of Iraq in 2003, where you can watch suicide bombings with powerful *anasheed* (religious songs) as accompaniment. These Muslims are true Muslims you are told. They have sacrificed their lives for the honor of Islam and the Muslims. These young martyrs are ensconced in heaven today for having made the greatest sacrifice for Islam. They are the model to be emulated, for what could be more selfless, noble, and moral than to give up your life for the greater glory of Islam?

The latest monstrosity of the Middle East is presented in its full enormity: the destruction of the Syrian people at the hands of the atheist, Kaffir, Baathi regime of Bashar al-Assad. You were very young when the so-called Arab Spring started in 2011. You knew that something was happening. You would catch glimpses of the news of massive demonstrations taking place in the central squares of a number of Arab capitals. These were revolutions. Tunisia was the first country to fall to the demonstrations. Its president fled. Egypt also had a revolution and its aging president was arrested and imprisoned. The Libyan leader was hunted down and killed in a gruesome manner. Yemen had an initially less violent outcome. And then all eyes were on Syria. The

Syrian people demonstrated and danced and demanded change.

Then Syrian children were arrested, tortured, and killed. Their bodies were returned to their families. More and more violence was committed against the Syrian demonstrators. You have grown up watching the daily reports of the deaths in Syria.

You also know that the destruction of Syria and the radical forces that are operating in the territory of northern Syria and Iraq have led to a great migration of refugees into Turkey and then across into Europe. Initially, the Europeans welcomed these refugees with open arms. Other refugees had already been established in enormous camps in Lebanon, Turkey, and Jordan. This new wave of refugees came across into Europe hoping for a better life than anything possible in the Middle East or North Africa. As Muslims, we watch these refugees risk life and limb to get away from where they originated. In fact, they are trying to get away from what are Muslim countries and Muslim lands. The debates that are taking place in Europe have gone from theoretical openness to a practical anger and panic over the implications of the influx. As Muslims we are upset that our fellow Muslims are no longer so welcome in Europe. But as Muslims, we are also facing the question of why our Muslim societies are breaking down across the Middle East—from Afghanistan to Libya.

You know that some of my work is concerned with the problem of Syria. You ask me when is it going to end. You seem to think that the world has left Syrians to their fate. Here the videos of tortured and maimed Muslim children are countless. The outrage you feel is completely rational, and justified. The crimes committed against the innocent and the defenseless are condemned by all people everywhere. But no one seems to be doing anything about it. Who is going to put a stop to the carnage? Who is going to take revenge against the killers? Every day in the Arab world, in Europe, and in the United States, you are told that governments are helpless in the face of global economic forces, or climate change, or extremism. Governments are not going to do anything because they do not want to or because they cannot. So the only one left is you. So what do you do? You are the only one who has an ounce of morality left. Only you seem to know the difference between right and wrong, between good and evil. There are others out there like you. They also feel the outrage. They feel the sense of impotence when they look at the way people seem to shrug at the news of the latest atrocity, and then get on with their mundane lives. Fast-food restaurants, TV shows, Facebook, and Instagram. You are all perplexed by the way people seem to be more interested in the petty politics of Congress and the European Union than they are by the greatest moral question of the twenty-first century. You, like human beings in general, have this constant urge to make sense of the world around you. It can be a painful process, but there is light at the end of this tunnel of worry, anxiety, and self-doubt. Could it be that the online ulema—or religious scholars of Islam—are correct? Could it be that they are the living embodiment of what Islam can and should and will become? The path is clear, the language is straightforward and simple. When all the clutter of modern life is removed, the path opens up before you toward meaning and purpose.

The more you look, the more you find what makes sense. You are all tapping into a great civilization. Or at least a civilization that was once great, and that must be great again.

You believe that your parents do not understand the issues you face. They live in a different world. They are content with the mind-numbing and backbreaking work they do. They are isolated and powerless in the face of technologies and economic forces. Can they even call themselves good Muslims? You are embarrassed to think it, but you cannot help it: your parents are cowards who do not want to face the world. They are not the good Muslims that you thought they were. Islam has demands and it has rights over us. We need to be good, and being good means living up to the demands of Islam. What are your parents doing? Nothing. They mutter things under their breath when the news comes on, they are always tired and irritable. They do not have any convincing answers to your questions. In fact, not only are they not living up to the clear and simple dictates of Islam, but they are also dinosaurs who have no role in this life. You love them, but they are peripheral in the great battle of Good against Evil.

There is a moment when you are faced with a key question. If you are serious about being a good Muslim, a proper Muslim, a true Muslim, then you need to live like one. What are the models for this? Actually, the model is there in front of you. It is the model of the Prophet Mohammed. You are told to emulate him. In every way. This is a noble and straightforward thing. The idea of following the example of a good and noble historical figure is not strange at all. In fact, you hear about the need for role models at school, at work, and in business. Many people are trumpeted as role models—scientists, actors, and singers. Of all the role models we Muslims have, the Prophet Mohammed is the finest.

Luckily, there is a long-standing tradition that outlines specific acts and sayings of the Prophet that allow you to fit yourself in smoothly. Some of the requirements, or at least what you are told are requirements, come across as quite strong, such as the need to distance yourself from non-Muslims entirely, and from Muslims who are not strictly observant. Soon, though, you join with others in expressing shock that such and such a person made what seemed to be an immoral joke, or that another Muslim was seen walking with a young lady who was not his relative. What could they be doing? you all wonder. And conclude that they must have been up to no good. Judgment of others comes quickly and easily. Why? Because you live a Muslim life of such high and demanding moral standards that everything around you seems ritualistically and morally incorrect. You find that you are living in a polluted world that needs radical cleansing.

There is a sense of peace and balance you feel as you join the communal prayer at dawn, or after work, and mostly on Fridays, when you pray our obligatory communal prayer of the week. You feel the dread as the sermon is over and the short prayer approaches its end. We all know the mosque to be a place of warmth and community. When we are far away from traditional Islamic societies, we feel a brotherhood and a sense of recognition when we gather in a mosque. The mosque in faraway places is a gathering place, a refuge, a place to sit with your community and Allah. The best moments are the Friday sermon and communal prayer. This is the time when the mosque is most full, and most welcoming. As soon as these moments pass, you know that you will be out in the cold or in dark streets, feeling a little lost and a little lonely. There is the emptiness as a new week builds up to the next Friday prayer. You are able to console yourself with listening to the captivating recitations of the Holy Quran that are freely available online.

What is special about the recitation of the Quran? The Angel Gabriel revealed the Quran to the Prophet Mohammed by reciting the verses to him and having him learn them by heart. Though you know the Quran as the beautiful leather-bound book with the wonderful calligraphy, the Quran is actually meant to be recited or read out loud. There are rules on how to read it out loud. The way it is recited today is the same way in which the Prophet recited it more than fourteen hundred years ago. In fact, today's reciters can trace their knowledge back through their teachers along a chain of people right back to the Prophet. So what you hear today is the way it has been preserved for hundreds of years. The recitations vary in quality, depending on the age and voice of the reciter. It's like being a musician. One reciter may have the technical mastery but lack in passion or emotional depth. You have your favorites. My favorite is the recitation of Al Sudais, the imam of the Holy Mosque in Mecca. You can listen to him for hours and feel the emotion of his love for Allah and his Message. Some of his recitations are recordings of him during Ramadan evening prayers. Here he sometimes breaks down in tears due to the emotion of the recitation. Others cry with him.

The recitations charge you up. They tap into a great river of emotion and energy. You are exhausted after listening. I am too. Sometimes I think that I should limit myself to listening for only an hour a week or an hour a day. Why? Because perhaps the intensity is too much. It jars with the outside world. Often I cannot manage the balance. The move from the beauty of the spiritual world to the ugliness of the outer world depresses me. You may feel the same way. As you know there is the beautiful story of Yousef, or Joseph, whose brothers were jealous of him and threw him down a well to his fate. It is a favorite chapter of the Quran because of the vividness of the story. We hear how he is rescued—into slavery—and how the women of the Pharaoh's court cut their hands because they were distracted by Yousef's beauty. We feel the injustice committed against Yousef, and we love the way life turns around for him. He becomes adviser to Pharaoh and is reunited with his father.

There are other chapters of the Quran that strike us with their calls to think and to contemplate the universe around us—from the mountains and the seas to the stars and the sun above us. And yet other verses call on the believers to defeat their enemies.

In all, between the verses of philosophical and spiritual contemplation and the verses of laws and action, we come away with a sense of the power and wisdom of Allah, and a renewed sense of the unity of the Muslim community.

The rhetorical effect, as well as the rhythmic pace, create a sense of peace and awe.

You become acutely aware of the dissonance between what you have just experienced—the word of Allah, unchanged and uncorrupted for over fourteen hundred years—and what surrounds you—rubbish in the streets, sullen looks of strangers, late-night rowdiness, meaningless conversations about sports, the housing market, and corrupt politicians. The Quran provides a stable reference point in a world of change, of turmoil, and of turbulence. We know how vigilantly generation after generation of Muslims has made sure that not one word or vowel has been changed in the text. The text has remained unchanged and perfectly preserved for hundreds of years. It is a stable point in the universe that we as Muslims can hold on to. This gives us as Muslims a sense of solidity and of certainty.

What better place than the warmth of prayer, the comfort of recitation, the certainty of moral worth? My generation knows this feeling too. It was my elders who headed off to Afghanistan in the 1980s to fight in a holy war of jihad against the atheist Soviet invaders. The

Afghans had a new leader take over in 1978 who was pro-Soviet. He started to introduce very big changes into Afghan society in the mistaken belief that he would be helping Afghanistan develop. The Afghan people are very tribal and devoutly Muslim. The changes put forward were too much. The Soviet Union sent in advisers, since Afghanistan shared big borders with it. Then they sent in the Soviet Army and got stuck in a war that lasted from 1979 till 1989. In 1980, the Muslim countries of the world condemned the Soviet invasion and began to plan action to support the Muslim country of Afghanistan. Lots of young Muslims from around the world started to organize and travel to Afghanistan. They and their Afghan brethren became known as the mujahideen—from the word *jihad*. *Jihad* is a word that can also mean "holy war." I was too young to go, but not too young to cheer for our brave warriors.

The world was divided clearly into that which was permitted and not permitted. Again, lots of parallels with the digital, binary world of the twenty-first century. Either something is good or it is not good, 1 or 0. Our Islamic ethics traditionally reflect this kind of approach. Simplicity. We find a mufti—the person who is allowed to make rules or provide religious advice and judgments—who has the correct credentials, and we either search his written opinions or ask him directly. Occasionally, the mufti seems to be talking about things that are not so relevant. Perhaps they are relevant and we have been focused on the wrong things all along. In any case, you have found a knowledgeable, qualified religious authority who knows what he is talking about. Over time, you will learn from him the proper way to be a good Muslim.

Quite often, this binary approach seems more appropriate to a different time and place. Sometimes you wonder whether there might not be another way in which we Muslims can be good Muslims and interact seamlessly with the multicultural, multicolored, multifragmented world that we actually live in. I know it is difficult to face uncertainty. It is more difficult for you in today's world than it was for my generation. We had less to be uncertain about. Many of us are now set in our ways. A little uncertainty can be put out of our minds. But you and your generation need to form your own ideas and your own approach to the world. Your world is more complicated, more volatile, more unpredictable. Why is this the case? The simplest answer is that the world is open to you through technology. There are no walls, no vast open spaces where nothing happens—as there were only a few decades ago. That is why many of you and your friends will try to lock into whatever certainty you can or that you find. The need to know that certain things are true is a human instinct. This is the desire for certainty. It is how we orient ourselves. It is how we give ourselves direction and protect ourselves. Certainty is the mental shell that pushes away doubt. The world you live in is different because the building of certainty requires more time, more knowledge, more experience, and more trust than ever before. Every child of your generation is in the same position, from the depths of Africa and Asia to the cities of North America.

You used to have friends of the opposite sex. Now you are taught that the sexes should be separated. This way there is no chance of illicit intercourse—that is, extramarital sex—taking place. You are initially a little surprised that there is an assumption that men and women are so likely to have sex the minute they are with each other. Perhaps it is the truth. You wonder whether there might be other problems that occur because of such a strict segregation. There are rumors of rampant homosexuality in societies that are so segregated that the opposite sexes almost never have the opportunity to interact the way they do in the liberal "decadent" West. Your friends from strictly Islamic countries seem to be relieved to be on holiday somewhere in the West. They breathe easier and seem more interested in sinning than praying.

They have stories to tell you about strict Islam. Stories about the way rules are enforced. In some strict Muslim societies, praying is not optional but enforced with a stick and a shove. In some strict Muslim societies, men must have beards for fear of punishment and in some cases death, and women must cover themselves up against their will. But you do not want to hear them or believe them. The Islam you know provides comfort and security. It is good and simple. They do not know what they are talking about.

Later I will try to answer the question whether it is more ethical to have a strict Islamic system or to have a psychologically healthy Islamic community. This question took years to evolve in my mind, but I think it is important for you and your friends to think about it before judging others.

Then there are the occasional questions that come up about such topics as slavery and war booty. How do these subjects make sense in the world in which you live? What about the astounding violence that is committed in the name of Islam around the world? Especially in the Muslim countries.

Islam is a religion of peace. We know this for certain. We greet each other with the phrase "al salam aleikum"—peace be upon you. Each chapter of the Quran starts with the phrase "in the name of Allah, the merciful, the compassionate." We often utter the same words when beginning an action, such as setting off on a journey or starting a talk.

So what kind of peace and when? And who decides?

Do you have anything to do with the decision? Is there a process for a decision to be reached? Perhaps we should just leave it to the scholars of Islam, the ulema, the guys we watch on those YouTube videos who speak confidently, and loudly, and know the answers.

I suppose in light of the arguments of some of the truly radical groups out there, Islam is a religion of peace, but I do not think we have quite worked out how. Is it because we cannot be at peace when others have declared war on Islam? That is the basic argument that the radical types make. They tell you and me that Islam is a religion of peace and beauty and prosperity as soon as it is allowed to be so. And as long as it has enemies plotting openly, and secretly, to destroy Islam, then we need to fight in a manner where the end justifies the means. Sounds like a fair argument. And I can tell you I have heard it every day in different forms in the Arabic language for more than thirty years. But what if there is a different way of thinking about it? What if we could live as Muslims in peace both with the non-Muslim and with the Muslim who is different from us in behavior and sometimes in belief? What if we can live in peace now? What would the Muslim world look like? What would we look like if we were not angry at our position in the world?

You are correct in thinking that if someone is going to change the world for the better, then it is you. I believe in you entirely and I think you can. I just want you to be aware of a few things before you embark on a course that might lead you down the wrong path. The binary world is not the only Islamic world you can live in. There is much more gray in between the black and white that the ulema and other scholars present us. And the gray is where you develop intellectually and morally. The gray area of uncertainty and doubt as to what is right and what is wrong is where you discover your own right to think for yourself and to participate in the construction of our ethical world in practice. This is where I believe you will be able to serve this world and the next—in being a thinking, ethically directed young Muslim.

There is much room to grow as individuals, and in doing so we can discover truths about our own inclinations. You should know that for every action, there is a reaction. Your perseverance, kindness, or humor creates a ripple effect in our culture just as much as your indifference, violence, or negativity. But in order to understand the Muslim individual, it is necessary to begin with an understanding of the Muslim landscape. It covers the Arab world and much of Southeast Asia as well as Central Asia and North Africa.

LANDSCAPES OF ISLAM

Saif,

You know that Islam is the religion of the Muslims, as revealed to us just over fourteen hundred years ago by the Prophet Mohammed. The Prophet lived in Mecca but had to flee to the nearby city of Medina with the early followers of Islam because the people of Mecca rejected the message of Allah. Soon, though, the followers of Islam grew in number and power and took over command of Mecca. These two cities are now the holy cities of Islam and are located in Saudi Arabia. You might not yet know about the different schools of Islam. You belong to the largest group within Islam, called the Sunnah or Sunnis. The Sunnis came into existence sometime after the passing of the Prophet when disagreements arose as to who should take up his position as head of the Muslim community. There were those who believed that the next leader should be a member of the family of the Prophet, and there were those who believed that the best man should be the next leader. In the end, the next leader was someone that many Muslims regarded as the most able to lead, and the fourth leader after the Prophet was a member of his direct family. Those who supported the family are now called the Shia, and those who supported the best man to lead are called the Sunnis.

When I say best man, the group around the Prophet—known as the *Sahabah*—were all men with the best moral qualities. Each had his own particular personality. I do not want to go into the detail of the disputes that have pursued the two groups through the centuries, because the Sunni-Shia divide is one of great stress for the Muslims of the world.

While you will hear loud voices on both sides denouncing the other, you should know that there is a vast number of Muslims on both sides of this divide who see the differences as minor and the joint faith as central. Given that there are said to be three hundred million followers of the Shia sect, and fourteen hundred million Sunnis, we must look forward to the day when Sunni and Shia clerics can put their differences behind them and thus remove the main obstacle to peace in the Middle East.

Beyond these broad groupings, you will be able to find all kinds of approaches within Islamic life. You will find Muslims like the Salafis, who copy every action ever recorded about the Prophet. Their worldview is that the only way to be a Muslim is by copying, or emulating, the Prophet. There is a powerful logic behind this. The Prophet was the Messenger of Allah. Who would know better than the Prophet what being a Muslim means? How do they know what he did in such detail? Through the Hadith, or the Sayings. This is a collection of what the Prophet said and did as recorded by those who witnessed him. This was a great communal effort to record that took place over the two hundred years or so after the Prophet passed away.

There are groups who contest which sayings are accurate and which are not. Already then you can see how Islam will evolve differently depending on what assumptions you accept. Within Sunni Islam, anyone who was a Muslim at the time of the Prophet can be consulted on what the Prophet said or did. Within Shia Islam, the circle of reliable sources is minuscule in comparison, including only the closest companions of the Prophet. It is like the difference between building your philosophy of life on the basis of a short story, or on the basis of a saga written over thousands of pages. Both are legitimate in principle, but they will lead to different outcomes. Both are facets of Islam.

Further differences appear between those who insist that they are the only ones who know the truth. This includes groups like ISIS, which you have heard about and are in Syria and Iraq. They have a very limited view of Islam based less on texts and more on a belief that Islam is about rules and punishments. For every error there is a punishment to be handed out. This makes sense to some Muslims because it fits their view of Allah as a lawgiver. And laws mean following the rules. Breaking the rules means punishment. However, they then take this idea further to imagine that every aspect of life falls under some rule. And therefore that there is a correct way to behave on every occasion no matter how small. The search begins to find out who has broken the rules. Before you know it, people live in fear not of Allah but in fear of those who have nominated themselves the enforcers of his rules.

At the other extreme—and if you travel farther west to Egypt, and to parts of North Africa—you will find the Sufis. The Sufis fall within the dominant Sunni branch of Islam, and they have a very different approach to worship. For them the spiritual aspect of Islam is the most important by far. For them worship is a form of love, and they find spiritual ecstasy in prayer and recitation. Violence and punishment are generally alien to their approach. Their approach to faith and life is one based on ancient spiritual techniques. Often regarded as mystically inclined, the Sufis do not play a significant role in the politically oriented types of Islam. And as we know, North Africa likewise suffers from the afflictions of Islamist extremism with which we are all very familiar. The color and philosophical variety in Islam is as wide and varied as human thought, whether Muslim or not.

And one question you will ask, if you are brave enough, is, What have they in common with each other? It's a question that will reappear. It is really a question about essence and identity. What is the essence of Islam? What is it that distinguishes Islam? What is it that makes you a Muslim or something else? The answer to this question will become evident through the letters you read here.

You need to know that the Islamic world can be divided by tradition, by philosophical belief, by politics, and by language. Even on the relatively small and sparsely populated Arabian Peninsula, it is possible to witness the presence of the easygoing and commercially oriented Muslims—in the coastal regions from the city port of Jeddah to the island state of Bahrain—alongside the ultrapuritanical adherents of what is commonly called Wahhabism. In the south of the peninsula, in Yemen, you will find an intellectually confident and philosophically coherent group in the Hadramout region. These Muslims are exemplified by the likes of Al Habib Ali Jafar, who can claim descent from the Prophet as well as being one in a chain of teachers and students from the time of the Prophet. These Muslims are often characterized by a serenity and wisdom that charms and surprises. Interestingly, the same region has produced some of the most violent and aggressive Islamists of the modern era. Hadramout is the homeland of Osama bin Laden as well as the area that houses Al Qaeda in the Arabian Peninsula.

In parts of Saudi Arabia as well as Kuwait, but particularly in Egypt, there is a much more politically oriented religious grouping known as the Muslim Brotherhood. The Muslim Brotherhood traces its origins to the ending of the caliphate in Turkey in 1924 by the reforming and secularizing Atatürk, and the decision of an Egyptian village schoolteacher to establish a movement in 1928 to reclaim the caliphate for Islam and create a form of Islamic world domination.

On the eastern coast of Saudi Arabia, as well as in Kuwait and Bahrain, you will find more than two million adherents of Shiism—historically the political opponent to the dominant Sunni branch of Islam. Iran is the leading political power espousing the Shia narrative of Islam. The adherents of Shia Islam are found in eastern Saudi Arabia, Kuwait, Bahrain, and Iraq. There are further gradations of Shia Islam such as the Zaidis of Yemen, the Ismailis of Pakistan, the Alawis of Syria, the Druze of Lebanon, and the Alevis of Turkey.

When you go farther, you will find that Islam has

deep roots in Pakistan—which was set up as a state for the Muslim populations of the Indian subcontinent after the British withdrawal from colonial India. India itself has a Muslim population of 180 million people. Farther east, in Indonesia there is a giant Muslim population of about 250 million people. Muslims have spread out across countries of sub-Saharan Africa, and even Russia has a population of 20 million Muslims. The diversity of Muslim ethnic backgrounds is one way in which Islam as a faith is enriched and reflected through languages and traditions across the globe.

When you think of Islam as a great and rich tradition, with a presence and roots across the globe, you feel proud. You are able to see that your religion, the religion of Allah, has a global presence. You think how remarkable it is that from the efforts of the Prophet Mohammed and his small group of early followers, a global religion has grown. And then you watch the news and you are shocked by the idea that Muslims are not welcome everywhere in the world. In fact, you discover something called Islamophobia. This is the "fear of Muslims." It is both a warning and an accusation. It is a warning for Muslims to stay away from places where there are not Muslim majorities, and it is an accusation in societies where everyone, including Muslims, are meant to be treated equally. We run away from places where we are told populations are Islamophobic. And we accuse democratic countries, where all are equal before the law, of being Islamophobic.

What do you do if you are a young Muslim facing this phobia?

Across the Arab world as well as in the United States and Western Europe, you will often hear that the bulk of the Muslim world is composed of peace-loving, moderate Muslims. And ideally, this is how it should be. Proponents of this position include people like Reza Aslan, Tariq Ramadan, and Abdullahi Ahmed an-Na'im as well as leading political figures like former president Barack Obama and former prime minister David Cameron. Aren't we peace-loving and moderate? Don't we know this for certain?

You will have the occasional doubt. I know you do, because we talk about it. We get lots of our news from the Internet and from the English-language TV stations. And terrorism and Islam seem to go together too often. I have spoken to my friends and some wonder who really does understand what Islam is about. How are you going to deal with this doubt? You are not on your own. It is a big question, and the adults are not doing very well answering it. Do we even know what "peace-loving" means?

In the wake of the June 2015 terrorist attacks in Sousse Beach, Tunisia, the prime minister asserted, "The people who do these things, they sometimes claim that they do it in the name of Islam. They don't. Islam is a religion of peace. They do it in the name of a twisted and perverted ideology that we have to confront with everything that we have."

His argument makes sense. At any one point in time, the number of extremists is remarkably small in comparison to the total number of Muslims in the world. However, an important factor behind the idea of Islam being a religion of peace is that proposing something that differs with such a description risks the promotion of Islamophobia.

Islamophobia is the unjustified targeting and demonization of Muslims for primarily political reasons. This is a serious matter and I completely support the fight against Islamophobia. Where I might differ is in the way the fight against Islamophobia conducted in the West affects the way we Muslims analyze and understand the dynamics within our own faith.

The debate that is of deep interest to the global Islamic community is currently taking place in countries from the United States to Russia, and in various Muslim states as well. The issue is whether to target the violence of radical Islam alone or to target the preparatory thinking and rabble-rousing that precedes the violence. The debate follows certain contours in the West due to the respect for freedom of speech and expression.

However, the debate in the Arab and Muslim

world—where such freedoms are viewed with trepidation, to say the least—takes a different course. Radicals spread their message in a way that has become second nature to us. You will often hear statements made in the local mosque or on the twenty-four-hour religious channels that mix the peaceful with the violent—and we are still only beginning to think about the consequences of this type of speech.

Can you imagine that there are 1.7 billion Muslims in the world today? Most hold traditional beliefs in tune with their local culture and history. This would be fine if the world of Islam were flat, but it might be more accurate for you to think of the Islamic world as a pyramid. The fundamentalist, reductive, "authentic" Muslims are at the top with the loudest voices and the clearest plan. So how is this going to affect you? Well, you need to begin thinking about how people use power in general and what they are using it for. It may seem a little early to have to think about these things, but there is a lot of power and influence at stake. And power tempts.

While it's true that only a tiny minority of extremists conduct themselves in a way that is inhumane or promote hatred and manipulate us into believing the world is fighting Islam, it is also true that their influence on the 70 percent of Muslims who are illiterate and the hundred million Arabs between the ages of fifteen and twenty-nine, of whom 28 percent are unemployed, must not be underestimated as we look ahead. Remember that the Arab world is the heartland of Islam, and so we should really be concerned about the quality of life of its populations.

The unfortunate reality for the rest of the world is that today's Arab youth will shape the character of the region over the coming years, and this could mean that we witness more anger and destruction, or productivity and progress, or a return to the traditional institutions of Arab and Islamic culture. Rigid job markets, out-of-date legislation, sectarianism, a weak productive identity, and finally, the oil price collapse that created a regional deficit of 9 percent of GDP in 2015 after years of surpluses are the extreme disadvantages troubling our youth. Unemployment is among the top three biggest obstacles facing the region (behind the rise of ISIS and the threat of terrorism). Opportunities for quality education at the university level remain weak. Only one of several hundred Arab universities was included in the 2015–2016 top 400 *Times Higher Education* World University Rankings. In addition to that, 8.6 million Arabs are not enrolled in primary or secondary school; 5 million of these children are girls.

These young Arabs will one day soon influence international politics and all global economies. How is the rest of the Muslim world faring?

WEALTH, OPPORTUNITY, AND REPENTANCE

Habeebie Saif,

The Arab world you were born into and have been brought up in is very different from what it was like fifty years ago. You recognize some of this when you meet older relatives who are unable to read or write, and who speak in an older, more distant dialect of Arabic. My father's generation—those born in the 1930s and 1940s—were born into a dry world with little food and water. There was no news to be had, and events like the Second World War were distant and marginal events in the life of the community. My uncle told me of how rice was hard to come by and that most of the time they lived off fish and dates. And even then, the bigger boys would be better fed, as they could grab more fish from the large communal tray on which their food was presented. The population of the Arabian Peninsula was small. In Abu Dhabi, where I spent my childhood, the population was a few thousand and there were no roads until the late 1950s. Then oil was discovered. It was initially discovered in Saudi Arabia in 1902, but it took years to begin production. Oil was discovered in the rest of the countries in the region in the 1930s and 1940s.

It was in 1973 that oil began to have a tremendous impact regionally and globally. This was the year when the oil-producing countries of the Arab world declared an embargo on oil supplies to the West. This meant that we stopped selling oil to countries like the United States, Canada, Japan, the UK, and the Netherlands. As a result the price of oil shot up. It skyrocketed, and thus the income of the oil-producing states rose drastically.

This huge increase in income allowed the oil-producing states to begin to invest in their local economies. Governments could afford to spend on roads, schools, hospitals, ports, and housing for all. This huge expenditure required people and companies to provide all kinds of services. As the economy grew, those who were lucky or well prepared made fortunes.

How does this affect the world you live in today? Oil wealth allows governments and wealthy individuals to back the interpretations they feel attached to. People in the Arabian Peninsula began to move from the traditional tribal scramble for survival to thinking about what they could and should do with the bounties of Allah. This is why we see so many wealthy families donating vast sums to build mosques and dig water wells for impoverished Muslim communities around the Islamic world.

Islamic interpretations coming out of the Arabian Peninsula—otherwise known as the Gulf Arab region—are dry and relatively harsh, a reflection perhaps of the desert environment. Life in the desert was tough and literally a place of black and white, with few colors and little diversity until the late 1950s, when oil wealth began to trickle down. Today's modern Arabian Peninsula is a far cry from the environment of the 1940s and 1950s. Many homes in the Gulf have countless coffee table books with glossy photographs of the pre-oil Arabian Peninsula. We see black-and-white photographs taken by adventurers like Wilfred Thesiger showing rake-thin Bedouins with long straggly unkempt hair looking incredulously into the camera lens. We hear from our elders of the intense harshness of life in the desert. Children and adults would die at the slightest sign of illness. Dysentery and diarrhea were frequent killers. I recently came across the photocopy of a notebook detailing the names, birth dates, and causes of death of a group of my relatives from 1850 to the 1940s. The vast majority died of forms of dehydration shortly after birth while others were afflicted much later in life.

The way we currently interpret our texts leaves little room for discussion or philosophizing and wondering.

Fifty years ago, you could go to mosque, read Quran, and then get on with your daily life by going to work, earning an income, and raising your family. Today it is possible to spend your evenings reading hundreds of fatwas, or collecting videos of suicide bombings or of executions of "enemies of Islam," or of atrocities committed by Westerners against Muslims in various countries of the broader Middle East. Or listening to very moving, hauntingly beautiful recitations of the Quran. This means that we are, each of us, able to intensify and magnify the emotions that we would normally feel. This of course applies across the entire spectrum of human interest, from pornography to gaming, from playing the stock market to doing research at a university. We become enclosed in a virtual world of inhuman emotional intensity. This pattern is repeated across the deserts of Arabia and the bedsits of suburban London, and the open fields of Rochester, Minnesota.

I remember how when my friends and I were children and teenagers, and then young men in our twenties, we would laugh, and also cry quietly, at the desires that we were faced with, and the commands not to lose our self-control. I had a good friend with whom I would pray during some years and whom I would accompany to wild parties in other years. Do I want to go into the details here? Not really, to be honest. Suffice it to say that my experiences showed me that people with a great desire to be good, and a great desire to experience life, can easily lose their way. My friend would oscillate with the regularity of a pendulum from one extreme to the other. One year he would be praying and visiting Mecca and repenting, and then he would appear drunk with his arms around a woman or two about to engage in revelry.

I think of this pendulum movement a lot. I experienced it myself in different ways. Many people I know personally, or know of, have gone through the debauchery-and-repentance cycle. It is not something specific to being a Muslim, or to growing up in a Gulf Arab country, or even in a Middle Eastern country. When I was in my teens, my mother introduced me to the classics of Russian literature. One of the greatest of Russian writers, Leo Tolstoy, was well known not only for his debauchery but for his repentance as well. The equally great writer Dostoyevsky was also a man obsessed with religion and questions of the divine, and yet he was a slave to his passions—particularly gambling.

I think that knowing of these people gave me a glimmer of hope that there was a possibility to avoid the pendulum movement. It became clear to me with the years that sinning, making moral mistakes, being weak in the face of desire, possibility, and temptation were all things that make us human. And it took me a few years, but I also realized that intense repentance and compensating for sins with greater piety could be just as destructive as the original errors.

I began to think that rather than torturing ourselves with guilt over these errors, there was the possibility of returning to a balanced, understanding middle zone. It is this zone that I think we are somehow lacking in our approach to Islam today. I want you and your generation to know that repentance should not be self-torture. Regret should not overwhelm you and force you into another form of intensity. Intensity distorts reality. And Islam in its essence is against the distortions of intensity.

There are now so many instances in which terrible crimes are committed by young men, and sometimes women, in the name of Islam. We are then told that the perpetrators were not particularly devout Muslims and that some of them were immoral from a Muslim perspective. Some of our Muslim leaders use this as an excuse to say that these people could therefore not have represented Islam—and this allows us to distance ourselves from the crimes. I think that we need to look at *Charlie Hebdo,* and the Bataclan, and Orlando and ask ourselves if this is not precisely what some of us are taught by our religious leaders. Is there not some truth to the idea that a strain of Islam welcomes repenters and born-again Muslims and asks of them to clear their sins by acts of great piety or fanaticism? We need to own up to the fact that we do not have mechanisms in place for the stray Muslim who wants to repent, or who wants to devote him- or herself to Islam in a sincerer manner than before. For some reason we have trained ourselves to "return" to our faith with an inhuman intensity.

How does this relate to our part of the world? I think that the historical sparseness of our environment, the harshness of our ancient physical existence, has clashed with the possibilities that wealth has given us. In our confusion, faced with choices and power, we cling to the older, more traditional solutions of repenting and being pious without a natural balance to hold us back.

We need to find a new balance that allows us to make our very human errors without needing to repent in a destructive manner.

FRAGMENTS OF MEMORY

Habeebie Saif,

I want to share with you my experience of growing up without a father in the Muslim world. In many ways it is similar to growing up in an environment where you are an outsider to what seems to be a homogenous community. Without a father, at an early age you become suspicious of those who would usurp your absent father's role. You are fearful and protective of whatever you are sure about. You prefer not to trust because you know that not trusting will take you further than trusting. In fact, when you feel you cannot trust anyone, you become aware of the positive power of trust and its force in society.

In Islam, we are given three days to mourn the passing of one of our own. After that, life goes on. Graves are generally unmarked—but if marked, then only with a stone—presumably to avoid unearthing the remains of others in preparation for a new grave. It always struck me as strong and courageous to leave the dead behind. For me, however, it has been impossible to leave my father behind. I have carried his memory with me through the years, always imagining what he might have said to me, or done in my place. And inevitably, I spent many years more than the permitted three days mourning his passing.

In all the years since my father's death in 1977, I have been collecting fragments of memory and weaving together a threadbare picture of the man. One of the key lessons I took from contemplating my father's life was the power of imagination, even in the most desolate of starting points. It has opened my eyes to how we build pictures of ourselves and others, to how we construct our personalities and those of others, to how we write our histories and the importance of doing so.

My father, Saif Ghobash, lived a short but fascinating life trajectory. He was born in 1933 to an elderly father, Saeed Ghobash, and a very young mother, Fatimah al Owaidh. The age difference between them may have been forty years or more. The environment in which they lived was extremely harsh, as it was across the area covered by the Emirates today.

Food was simple. Dates for breakfast, rice and fish for

other meals, although since food was often prepared communally, this meant that there was a battle between the stronger and the weaker to get the fish.

His siblings were much older than he was. The youngest was older than him by twenty-five years. The oldest was thirty-eight when my father was born; his name was Mohammed Saeed Ghobash. He had been the first person from the region—vaguely defined—to have traveled to Egypt to enroll at Al-Azhar University. This was a journey that required passage through Syria, down through Palestine and Jerusalem in the late 1920s and through to Cairo.

My grandparents are said to have died within a few months of one another. My father was likely twelve at the time. This is when he inherited two slaves and a plot of land. I met a former slave of my grandfather's when I was eighteen; he was in his late eighties and had long been given his freedom and was still living in the house provided to him by the family. Though slavery was common in the region in the early part of the twentieth century, life was harsh for all, and slaves were more often than not treated as part of the family. My father made the decision to free his slaves based on his own sense of morality. But as tradition would have it, this caused severe problems, as they were not sure what to do with the new found freedom. The man I spoke to that day told me that he had been purchased with his mother while he was still in her womb.

The reason I recount these details is to underline how different and how tough life could be in the Gulf in the early part of the twentieth century; it also demonstrates how far we have managed to progress from such humble beginnings. Much of what we know of Islam in the Arabian Peninsula was formed and polished in this tough desert environment. You should know this when you think of how Islam works in a world of malls and iPhones and holidays around the world.

The world of the Arabian Peninsula was very small in the 1950s. People knew who was traveling and when. They knew the names of all the tribes and subtribes. People oriented themselves by knowing who was married to whom and who was related to whom. You know this still matters today, but it is not as prevalent as it used to be. The states along the Gulf were all connected by family and trade. The beautiful traditional boats or dhows that you know from the port of Dubai used to ply the trade routes up and down the Gulf.

Your grandfather found work in an engineering office in the neighboring state of Kuwait. Here, my father and his colleagues were invited by another employee in the office to start an organization for Palestinian liberation. At the time the Palestinians were only a few years into their attempt to organize themselves after the establishment of the state of Israel in 1948. In the cozy world of the 1950s, the colleague was a man called Yasser Arafat, and he was establishing something that he wanted to call the Palestinian Liberation Organization. This organization became the standard-bearer for the Palestinian people. And my father would later come across Yasser Arafat in the course of his work.

For reasons unknown to me, my father did not join or participate in the establishment of the PLO. This simply illustrates how small and intimate the community of educated Arabs was at the time. It also tells you that the thinking then was not religious; it was national and social. It was about people and their rights, and not about religion and power over others. This comes later.

A friend of my father encouraged him to think of moving to Germany. Job prospects seemed good. He finally settled for up to six years in Düsseldorf.

The lack of information, and therefore clarity, about these years is very frustrating. It is near to impossible to know what my father did and how he thought at this time. What was he doing in Germany? What was he planning to do? The only surviving remnants of his time in Germany are a few photographs from the early 1960s as well as an address and a large number of books in German. I would often look through his books to try to understand what he was interested in, what he was driven by.

Finally, my father decided to move on, and as luck would have it, the Soviet government had established a scholarship system for Arab students. My research tells me that approximately two thousand Arabs benefited from the scholarships over the lifetime of the program. My father enrolled at Leningrad Polytechnic in what is now Saint Petersburg in 1964 and graduated in 1968 with a Russian wife—my mother, Lioudmila Alexandrovna Blagoveshenskaya.

My mother was born to Alexander Blagoveshenskaya and his first wife, my grandmother, who died in 1945 at the age of thirty, approximately. My mother had a younger half-brother, Valerii, and a stepsister, Valentina. They grew up in the industrial city of Rybinsk, the regional capital of Yaroslav Region just north of Moscow. After graduating from school my mother worked in a chemicals factory for three years before enrolling in the same university as my father. They met while studying engineering and married in 1968. A cousin of mine recently found me on Facebook and recounted that he had tried to find out more about the family history. He managed to ascertain that many of our male relatives had been Orthodox priests who had been killed by the Bolsheviks in 1918.

In a strange way, my parents' lives were similar to the extent that they were born in relatively poor circumstances, in marginal areas of the regions where they grew up. They benefited from government scholarships and money lent by family and friends over the years.

Soon after they married, my parents made their way back to the Emirates—which were still regarded as under British control. Oil had already been discovered in Abu Dhabi, and there were rumors that there might be hydrocarbons in the other Emirates. My parents went to Ras al Khaimah, which was experiencing a property boom of sorts as wealthy Gulf Arabs from Kuwait, Bahrain, and Saudi Arabia bought land in anticipation of the discovery of oil.

Interestingly, oil was never found in commercial quantities in the Northern Emirates and so many speculators from the late 1960s and early 1970s still own large swathes of land in Ras al Khaimah. My father found himself a job in the local municipality as an engineer. Over the years he had learned a number of languages including English, Russian, German, and classical Arabic.

He soon found himself working part-time in the entourage of the ruler of Ras al Khaimah at the time— Sheikh Saqr bin Mohammad al Qasimi. In 1971, the United Arab Emirates was formed of six Emirates along the coast of the Arabian Gulf, which lies opposite the coast of Iran. As these developments preceded the Iranian Revolution, Iran was still ruled by the

Mohammad Reza Shah Pahlavi of the Iranian monarchy. The British had made it clear that they were intent on leaving the area and so had assisted the Emirates to unite and form a federal government. Ras al Khaimah only joined the federation in 1972, as the seventh member of the UAE.

When the UAE was formally announced in 1971, Iran immediately invaded three islands belonging to both Sharjah and Ras al Khaimah. My father was included in the group led by the ruler of Ras al Khaimah when they visited Tehran to negotiate the status of the islands with the shah of Iran. This seems to have been my father's first official involvement with foreign affairs. Shortly after Ras al Khaimah joined the federation, my father was appointed undersecretary in the Ministry of Foreign Affairs in Abu Dhabi, the UAE capital. In 1974, he was promoted to the position of minister of state for foreign affairs with a seat in the UAE Cabinet of Ministers. In quick succession, in 1968, 1969, 1971, and 1972, my siblings and I were born.

I was born in 1971, the same year the United Arab Emirates was founded, which has always been, to a certain degree, a point of pride and symbolic of my sense of self.

THE LIMITS OF WHAT
WE CAN KNOW

Dearest Saif,

The United Arab Emirates was a country formed
from the tribes around the tip of the Arabian Peninsula.
The tribes were divided between those that were desert
dwelling and those that were seafaring. They had
historically fallen under the control of the British, who
wanted to ensure safe passage from Britain to India, and
so Britain set up something called a protectorate. This
effectively meant that we were under British rule, with
few if any direct material benefits.

As a historical entity, the UAE was not burdened by
the Arab-Israeli conflict or the history of the region in
any way similar to other Arab nations. The Emirates
had a clear sense of identity; we were marginal but
determined survivors, and our culture, although young,
was very strong. It is, as it always has been, a country
that has genuine concern about the well-being of its

citizens and residents. Though the formula for wealth distribution has changed from land grants in the 1970s to economic opportunities and jobs for all, the focus has always been on the Emirati individual—an Emirati individual with a character, a personality, and an identity. But looking back, the truth is that few people expected the Emirates to survive, let alone succeed in the manner that it has.

Terrorism struck the Emirates for the first time on October 25, 1977. I attended an English-language school just down the road from our home. As the country was still undergoing tremendous investment and building, there were many foreign contractors, and this is why there were a number of English-language schools. My siblings and I were sent to one, as the quality of education was much higher than in the Arabic-language schools. I remember the day when I was abruptly pulled from class. My siblings and I were told there would be a three-day holiday and we celebrated. Back at the house, however, we returned to find my mother crying. Men stood in small circles outside in the garden. The women remained inside to watch a funeral broadcast on the family television. It was an old television with knobs and wooden shutters. The house was crowded, hot, and I have a vague recollection of everything feeling saturated by tears. An Emirati flag covered the coffin. I asked whose funeral it was but received no answer.

Many years later I realized it was my father's funeral. Over the years I have spent many hours trying to piece together his life story. It has proved more difficult than might have been expected. The journey has been revealing and instructive, even though the facts of his life still remain hazy and in many cases simply unknown.

The process of thinking about his life has opened up other areas for me personally. In attempting to come to grips with a father who was absent through violence committed in a political context, I have been exposed in a direct manner to the way in which we investigate matters. The limits of what we are permitted to know and what we can know. The boundaries of legitimate questioning and the self-imposed silence on the assumption that certain thoughts should not be expressed. In our part of the world, we have yet to evolve legal mechanisms that would allow for reviews of government or police action, or a third-party investigation into police performance. There is no clear mechanism to gain further information from government bodies. These legal mechanisms are developed as societies progress.

When I was able to gain a certain perspective on this tragedy, the questions I had as a result of it became a rich source to be mined. It has allowed me to think of how we collect facts and whether we are even allowed to collect facts. There are choices in how we write our histories—whether personal or public histories. What do we do when we simply do not have the facts? What do we do when there are glaring gaps in the life story we are attempting to rebuild? We begin to imagine what might have been the case, what a person would have or could have logically thought. We begin to project something of our own character into the person we are rebuilding.

MY FIRST DARK DAYS

Saif,

The summer of 1977 was wonderful. We went on a cruise liner around the Mediterranean and the Black Sea. We swam and played on board in the sun. We strolled around different port cities and we met my Russian grandparents in Odessa. I have clearer memories of this short holiday than of many experiences I have had since.

We came home to Abu Dhabi in the Emirates at the end of summer and went back to school. Then came the day when my younger brother and I were brought back home. Then my older brother and sister were flown home from boarding school. Then my mother sat us down and told us that our father had "died" and was not coming back. I remember my younger brother and I did not understand what "died" meant and so we were told that he had gone away to a place called heaven.

Would he be coming back? We were five and six years old respectively. I thought to die was a temporary act and as soon as it was completed, my father would be returning—sort of like going to the office or going shopping. My younger brother had even less of an idea of what was going on, but we were both certain that nothing serious had happened.

On the day of his assassination, your grandmother recounts, he stood at the top of the stairs and told her that he had been called to see off the Syrians at the airport and that it was an unexpected request. "I am not meant to be seeing him off," he said. "I have other things to do today." But he dutifully complied. My mother says he looked angelic that day. That there was an aura around him. Perhaps it was hindsight, but she speaks of having had a feeling, a premonition of something that was about to happen.

He headed to the airport and met with the other officials and visitors. In the airport entrance, shots rang out. Amid the panic, it was alleged that his loyal driver dragged him to the car. The person who killed him was a nineteen-year-old Palestinian gunman. My father had become the direct victim of inter-Arab gun politics as it related to the Palestinian Question and the Assad regime of the 1970s and their brutal massacres of Palestinian refugees.

I learned in short conversations scattered haphazardly

over the years what that day meant for people. The news came out fairly quickly that the assassin was a Palestinian. This caused anger and in some cases rage among my fellow Emiratis. This was for a host of reasons. The UAE, under the presidency of Sheikh Zayed bin Sultan al Nahyan, founder of the UAE, had always been a tremendous supporter of the Palestinian cause and the Palestinian people. The UAE had donated large sums to the Palestinian cause and had opened its doors to many Palestinians so that they could work and live in the UAE.

My father had been a vocal and committed supporter of the rights of the Palestinians and had been heard making impassioned speeches at the UN General Assembly meetings in New York. For him to be assassinated, and by a Palestinian, was a cruel irony and cause for anger. One close Palestinian friend of my father told me that anyone not wearing traditional Emirati clothing was at risk of being beaten by Emiratis wanting to take revenge. He himself found he was unable to attend the funeral prayers in honor of his close friend due to fear. Similar feelings were expressed by others.

The papers were covered with the news. Page after page of photographs and minute descriptions were provided. The clearest memory I have is the photograph of the windows partially shattered by the bullets. There were black circles drawn around the holes on the hazy photos. The number of shots was counted. The location of the shooter was outlined in another photograph on the first-floor landing. He had shot from above and down into the group as they walked through the main doors to the airport terminal.

I read and reread the papers from October 26, 1977, and of the few days that followed. As a child I was eager to know what happened. I wanted to know every detail. I wanted to know why and how and what and where, and then why again. I saw these newspapers for the first time in 1983 when I was twelve years old. The emotional impact was heavy. I read the newspapers over the course of a few days. Then I repacked them into the steel suitcases in which they had been stored by my mother for safekeeping.

Over the next few years, I returned to them. I would notice a few more details as well as a few more missing elements. No mysteries were solved but they left a set of impressions on me. It became very clear to me as the years passed that the picture created by the papers over the course of a few days showed that a man's life can be ended brutally—without warning for reasons he could not have guessed. Even in his last few moments of life, I can only imagine that my father would not have guessed at a reason for why he had been shot that day. In fact, he might be surprised if he knew that in 2017, almost forty years after his death, his widow and his children still cannot make sense of it. It is in a certain respect a comedy of deathly errors that involve a young Palestinian man with a gun and a target, but who does not recognize which of the two men in suits of the same height and build is the man he has been sent to kill.

It is with bitterness that I think of other instances where a lack of training and education lead to tragedy in the Arab world. I am telling you this family history not just because it is part of your history also. I am telling you because your grandfather's killing has made me very aware of all the other places where we use violence in order to get what we want. There is a way in which violence is a part of our lives, and we cannot deny it. This is what you need to think about and question why.

Years later I was at an Abu Dhabi hospital seeing a doctor who had known my family for years. He took out a pen and paper and began to sketch a heart with a torn coronary artery. This was the damage done by one of the bullets to my father. Some people have told me what his last words were alleged to have been, but there seems to be no way of really knowing. It is fascinating how people invent events and utterances in the hope that they will make you feel better. From what I gather, my father lost so much blood that he could not have survived the car ride to the hospital. I can only guess at this stage, as there are differing accounts as to who actually pulled him from the scene and who drove him to the hospital that day. It has made me very aware of how people report things, and how people will differ when recounting the smallest of events. This is something you need to be aware of when you hear people stating with certainty what happened centuries ago.

My father's life ended in violence. This violence destroyed him. When I was twelve and reading the newspapers from the day following his shooting, I felt that this violence was the only violence that existed. Only the violence committed against my father had any presence, any meaning for me. Clearly it was violence that outlived its moment and passed through across the years. What surprised me and continues to move me to action is that this violence has imprinted itself across my mother and siblings' lives, and the lives of you and your brother. Because I was six when my father died, I remember how, when you turned six years old, you worried for the entire year that I would die just as my father had died.

Each of us has at the back of our minds the horror of passing before our children have matured to a position of independence and wisdom. We think of leaving home and not coming back to you. Of course, this feeling requires a decisive intervention. The short way out of this is to accept that violence occurred and that violence can reoccur. Accidents happen. Life happens. But it is not enough. I need to write to you now with all that I can give you and tell you. Even if it only begins to make sense to you years from now.

I myself did not realize the prevalence of violence in our societies immediately. In fact, it took years. It kind of trickled into my consciousness.

The broader realization that we are surrounded by violence in the Arab world struck me later—when I was eighteen and Saddam Hussein invaded Kuwait. This is when we began to hear detailed descriptions of violence being committed against people who were like us in the Emirates. The violence took place in a context that had only been hinted at up until this point in 1990. The rhetoric of Arab media and schooling had been that the Arabs were one people and one nation, bound by one language. The Arab world has been gripped by the idea that we are a people of different origins, tribes, and ethnicities but brought together by speaking the same language. There has been a dream of uniting the Arab world from Morocco on the Atlantic Ocean to Oman on the Indian Ocean.

The states of the Arabian Peninsula—except Yemen, which has little oil and a large population—enjoyed an economic boom throughout the 1970s and the 1980s because of the high price of oil and the immense infrastructure that needed to be built. Throughout the 1980s, however, Iraq was at war with Iran—in order to prevent the Iranians from extending their influence across the region. This was seen by many as Iraq defending the Arab Gulf states. Once the Iran-Iraq war ended in 1988, the Iraqi government was heavily indebted and demanded funds from the Gulf states in order to rebuild. Kuwait shares a border as well as oil fields with Iraq. The Iraqi leader of the time, Saddam Hussein, decided that the Kuwaitis had been stealing Iraqi oil from these joint fields. With a great deal of fist waving and threats, he demanded compensation.

Then Saddam Hussein did what no one ever expected. He invaded Kuwait.

Violence again, and between Muslim countries, again. The invasion of Kuwait in 1990 and the general euphoria about this in the non-Gulf Arab states clarified for Gulf Arabs the hatred of those less fortunate than us. Parties were held in some expatriate homes in the remaining Gulf states celebrating the comeuppance of the Kuwaitis. The PLO backed the invasion. Public demonstrations took place in Jordan, Yemen, and southern Lebanon in favor of Saddam Hussein as the savior and liberator of the Arab people—presumably from Israel and the petro-states. This physical violence expressed political positioning and political positions. Violence made clear who was friend and who was foe. It made clear that one of our defining elements is how others define us. Defined as wealthy, oil-rich, ignorant desert Arabs, we were condemned by the Arabs of the less fortunate parts of the Arab world with much higher populations and much less wealth. The invasion of Kuwait and its subsequent liberation was a milestone for Gulf Arabs of my generation. It was when we came face-to-face with the idea that other Arabs and other Muslims did not like us. This is when we realized that we were no longer in our villages and our traditional towns. Now, the Gulf Arab world had entered the center stage of world affairs. Though oil was a great resource and provided us with funds to build our countries and educate our people, it was also a geopolitical obsession for poorer countries and more populous countries both near and far. Whether we wanted to be or not, we were relevant.

A few years after the invasion of Kuwait when I was fresh out of university, I picked out a short history of the Arab world written by a well-known author. It began by defining the real beginning of the Arab world at the point when the Prophet Mohammed received his message. The author went on to consider how the Arabs were from then on the best of all peoples, races, and nations—thanks to Islam. He then surprised me by briefly looking at the Arabs before the onset of Islam and declared them also to have been the best of peoples, races, and nations—in comparison with the Persians and the Romans, who allegedly practiced incest and were generally morally despicable and corrupt. As the years passed, I repeatedly came across the sensation that we Muslims were not being awfully truthful or objective about our past. Surely we could not have been perfect from the beginning of time until today? You will recognize this theme in many of your discussions with your colleagues. The theme is that we are the best, that we must be united, and that this way we will be victorious over our enemies. I think you are fully justified in listening to this narrative. You will find that the narrative of we Muslims being the best is a powerful one and that you are not allowed to think that perhaps we are not the best at the moment. This has a lot to do with statements in the Quran to that effect as well as sayings of the Prophet. It always makes me feel uncomfortable when I am told this by someone who is clearly not the best, nor making any effort to raise himself from the low place where he has settled. Sloth, arrogance, and ignorance are not virtues of the best. So this is a place where we can state clearly that Allah may intend for us to be the best, and may demand that we be the best, but that ultimately this is not something we have lived up to yet.

I also think you are fully justified in finding it odd, and perhaps a little surprising, as you travel the world and do not see so clearly that people are out to get you. I also think you will often recognize that though you are a Muslim, and a member of a global community of Muslims, you disagree not just with some of them, but with a lot of them. And you may feel guilty for these thoughts. Don't feel guilty. What you are experiencing is the same set of facts from the perspective of a different mental universe. I am talking about the special mental universe that lies in your head. And rest assured that Islam has the tools and the flexibility to guide you through a world where areas of gray predominate.

I used to think that answers being either black or white was a blessing. But after a while they seem inadequate. Remember that the answers that are so cutting and decisive are not the answers that Islam is giving, but the answers that a "knowledgeable" person with a background in the written material is giving.

You and your friends engage in this type of activity all the time. Every time you leave a cinema and you discuss the film you have just watched, each of you will have a slightly different take on the movie. The characters will be seen differently, the story will be understood differently by each of you. Some of you will have stepped out of the cinema for a few minutes and thus missed a crucial piece of information that holds the film together. Others will have dozed on and off, not particularly taken by the story. Each of you can be said to have watched the film, and the film has not changed in any way. In fact, the film is unchangeable. But each of you has taken the film on in a different and particularly individual way. And for each of you the film is actually a different experience.

My point here is that differences will occur, and they will occur in the places that you have been taught to expect clarity and consistency.

Life is diverse. Living is to live with difference. Anyone telling you that difference should be stamped out is stamping out life. Those people insisting that there are black and white answers to the difficult questions are stamping out the diversity that is inherent in life.

WHO ON EARTH TOLD YOU THAT?

Habeebie Saif,

Where does religious knowledge come from? Who has the right to talk about Islam? You will discover lots of people telling you what to do and when to do it. I want you to be polite, but demand respect for your mind and independence of will. If what someone tells you sounds convincing, ask more questions. In today's world, take more than a step back. There are many things to consider. Stay strong and do not hand your fate to others.

I remember watching TV with my father when I was about six years old. Someone was reciting the Quran on the small screen. It was late afternoon. He was dressed in the traditional clothing of a graduate from the ancient center of Sunni scholarship—Al-Azhar University. He had a gray coat with small buttons done up all the way to his chin. You could hardly see his neck. On his head, he wore the famous Al-Azhar turban with a thick white band and a ruby red flat top. His eyes were closed in deep concentration and he held his right hand up to cup his right ear. He rocked gently back and forth. As he chanted the verses of the Quran, I turned to my father and I asked him if the man on the screen was Allah. My father smiled at me and told me that Allah was not visible to us, and that the man on the screen was not Allah.

I did not yet realize that Allah, or God as he is known in other religions, was not embodied in human form. I assumed that Allah was visible to all and that I would see him one day.

This little memory makes me think of the occasions when people around us take on the authority of Allah, and demand thoughts and actions of us as though they were either Allah or his representatives on earth.

I want you to be on the lookout for people who talk with unerring conviction and authority about what others should do. Especially about what others should do. These are the people who always seem to lead us into some kind of trouble. You will no doubt know the kind of person I am talking about. In school, on the playground, it is the boy or girl who sets the rules of the game with the loudest voice and a bit of bullying. And who then proceeds to modify the rules whenever they concern their own behavior. This is the kind of behavior that you will also notice when it comes to religion.

The funny thing about those who claim authority in matters of religion is that they often make excuses for their own behavior because they have "devoted" themselves to the work of the Divine, and therefore, there is some kind of implicit leeway or permission for them to be "weak" on occasion. This has been seen in news about jihadists drinking alcohol and visiting bars for adult entertainment, as well as in the sexual scandals of the Catholic Church or the photos that we have seen of Buddhist monks traveling by private jet to oversee their fortunes. Of course, I do not mean to condemn all men and women of religious devotion. On the contrary.

What I am saying to you is that you need to make sure that you understand that those with plausible authority are also human beings like you and me. They are human beings, who can and will be distracted by the traditional human temptations of power, money, and sex. When I was a child, I was always willing to inflate the authority of such people, based simply on the fact that they carried themselves with authority. They had special uniforms. They had specialized knowledge. They spoke with a weariness that must have come from deep thought and great suffering. They spoke to us in a mystical manner. We would not understand everything they said, because we were simply not wise enough or good enough to understand.

The aura of authority can serve as a cloak for earthier matters. I want you to be aware of this possibility. This is a very human weakness of those who are looking for certainties in an ever changing world. We have a desire to know and believe that there are truly good people somewhere nearby. When we think we have found such a person, we are tempted to grant them our respect and even love. We slip into adding qualities to them that other observers can see they do not possess. Beware about endowing others with a goodness they do not have. Recognize that the goodness you see in them may actually be your own goodness. Turn your eyes inward to your own goodness and recognize that for what it is worth.

The question of authority is common to all religions. It spreads wider to encompass the workplace, school, and university, and anyplace where humans interact.

There is always someone who claims to know better than the others. Over the course of my life, I have gone from gullibly believing those who claim this authority in front of the group to having a more realistic view. I want you to make this move quicker than I did. We are often advised to give someone the benefit of the doubt. Or we are told that someone has a good heart deep down and thus we should not judge this person on the basis of their outward behavior. Or that the person in question is so learned that only those who have come close to learning as much will ever truly understand the wisdom attained.

The other side of this relationship is that you are told that you do not have the authority to speak on certain matters. Again, you will find this in all spheres of life, including the sphere of religion. The acquisition of authority by one person usually correlates with a removal of authority from the other person. Here you will be told that you should simply fall in line, follow orders, be a team player, do your job, focus on what you can do, and leave more serious matters to others.

WHAT IS TRUE ISLAM?

Habeebie Saif,

As you experience the world of Islam, you will notice that people will talk about Islam in at least two significant ways. They will often talk about Islam in a way that makes you think that Islam is something that exists somewhere in a perfect form, as though somewhere else. This is what we hear referred to as True Islam, or Islam the way it was before weak and foolish human beings added all kinds of innovations and distortions to it. This is a very abstract understanding of Islam. It suggests that there is an Islam that exists and has meaning without people practicing it. I find this difficult to comprehend.

The other way in which we refer to Islam is when we talk about the way in which Islam is practiced in the community to which we belong. What might be another way of thinking about this idea of True Islam?

Perhaps we might realize that Islam is less a set of doctrines that operate like a machine. Perhaps we should consider the idea that Islam's truth expresses itself differently in different cultures, in different geographies, and in different times. Rather than thinking there is only one version of Islam that all Muslims should conform to, as some suggest, we should look around ourselves and discover the multiple ways in which people take up Islam. Rather than thinking in black and white, we should think with all the colors of the rainbow and see Islam as a morally and ethically rich faith. The black-and-white approach is one that sets Muslims in conflict with one another needlessly and robs us all of our humanity. Why? Because in refusing the validity of other cultural approaches to the Islamic faith we reject what makes us special and beautiful. So look to Central and Southern Asia for enlightenment on how local tradition mixes and interacts with Islam. Look to the inner cities of the United States to see what Muslims do and say there. Look to the campuses of universities around the world and listen to how academics relate their Islamic faith to cutting-edge philosophical methods. Islam is not the property of the Arab world. Islam belongs to us all.

This approach sees Islam as a set of principles grounded in the humanity of the Quran and the wisdom of the Prophet. So that each community, each group, and each person has the freedom to reexpress this Islam in accord with the environment that they are in. This approach might even allow for those seeking to actively spread Islam to see greater success. Rather than seeing the spread of a narrow range of behavioral patterns more suited to the seventh century, or the tenth, we would see the spread of the Islamic values of respect, care for others, humor, generosity, and the search for knowledge and justice.

When we see Islam as a set of values capable of being expressed through local cultures and practices, then we do not need to fight over who controls its definition. Islam then fades into the background as a set of principles common to the deepest humanity.

These presentations and claims around True Islam are part of the problems that we face today as Muslims. Why is this so? If you think about it a little longer, if you think that there is a True Islam, then there must be a False Islam. This kind of thinking makes me feel very uncomfortable. If we go around declaring certain actions and thoughts to be True Islam, and others to be not True Islam, or False Islam, how will we ensure that we are the ones who are right? And what happens if we are on the wrong side of this relationship?

There are very aggressive groups throughout Islamic history who have declared that they were in possession of the knowledge that gives birth to True Islam. The

Khawarij of the seventh century were one such group. What did they do that was relevant to the issues we face today? They declared that those who claimed to be Muslims but differed from the Khawarij in small details of belief and practice were infidels, or nonbelievers. The Khawarij thus claimed to be in possession of the Truth. This approach to the Truth is what persists in important parts of today's Islamic world.

ISIS is the terrorist group that declares its expression of Islam is the True Islam that people imagine exists somewhere. Observe what happens to those who differ even a little in their beliefs from those held by ISIS leaders. They are punished, they are thrown off buildings, they are burned alive, they are killed in myriad ways.

When we declare the Truth as something that we know, and possess, it creates a dynamic of its own. If the Truth exists, then it means that there is a clear answer to every question. It means that religion answers every doubt, and every shade of gray is converted to black or white, halal or haram, permissible or not.

I think that this approach presents a serious danger to all those within the Islamic faith who are trying to expand the notion of what it means to be human within the bounds and parameters of that faith.

"ISLAM IS A RELIGION OF PEACE"

Habeebie Saif,

In reading the newspapers or watching the news, you will have come across the phrase "Islam is a religion of peace." Every time a violent act is committed by Muslims in the West, or a terrorist act is connected to Muslim perpetrators, someone from the Muslim community will appear in public stating that Islam is a religion of peace. In the Arab world, we hear the same phrase repeated. Great scholars of our religion state it again and again. Leaders of countries make this statement.

It seems a simple statement. Why should Islam or any religion be anything other than peaceful? The idea of religion and peace seem to go hand in hand. It would sound wrong if we said that we have a religion of war, or a religion of anger, or a religion of violence. So why do I get uncomfortable every time I hear the phrase "Islam is a religion of peace"?

You know I do not like statements that do not take us anywhere. A statement like "Islam is a religion of peace" is simply that: a statement. It does not explain anything to you or me. It does not explain why violence is often committed in the name of Islam. It does not tell me how we express our Islam in a manner that is peaceful. When I hear the phrase, I burn with the desire to know where we go next. What do we do with this peaceful religion of ours?

Well, in this letter to you today, Saif, I want to explore with you some of my ideas and some of my questions about peace within Islam. I hope that by exploring some of these ideas and questions, we can both come to a better understanding.

I hear the statement and I imagine the next lines. "Islam is a religion of peace, because we no longer live in the Middle Ages and we do not think that religions need armies and borders to defend themselves. It is a religion of peace because Islam is a state of mind and grace, rather than a team of warriors who can only look at the world from their self-defined perspective as warriors. Islam is a religion of peace because if we are to think of ourselves as a group, then we are an ethical group, not a military group. And as an ethical group or community, we work in the world through ethical behavior, not military tactics or prowess. Islam is a religion of peace because to be otherwise is to make a mockery of our Prophet's legendary care and kindness. Islam is a religion of peace, not because elderly scholars or smooth public spokesmen tell us that it is, but because we live it every day in a manner that reflects calm, self-possession, discipline, and attention to the needs of others."

Perhaps an extended statement like this would make me feel better about Islam as a peaceful religion.

Saif, please think about why Islam is peace as opposed to violence, anger, frustration, war, and destruction.

Some people will say that Islam is a religion of peace, but that it is also a religion that is under attack from non-Muslims, or the West, or imperialism, or Zionism, or capitalism. In fact, as Muslims we are told daily through various media that we are under attack by those who fear our strength or our potential. We are then told that these attackers are the reason why we must unite as a global Muslim community and fight back. How we fight back is a question that is left unanswered, and so certain people take the opportunity to define the fight back as one that is personal, violent, and random.

What should we do? Why does this make us feel uncomfortable? If we are Muslims and our religion is one of peace, then why are there loud voices that have declared that we are at war? And that this war is one that has enemies everywhere and all the time? The lack of clarity is upsetting. If we follow this path, then we will be at war with all people for eternity. This cannot be the correct approach to life in the service of Allah.

If we are a religion of peace, then surely we should react to perceived threats with an open heart and open hand. Perhaps instead of calling for war by all, in all places and at all times, we should call for trust, care, and generosity by all, in all places and at all times. To my mind, this reaction to a perceived threat would be more consistent with the statement that Islam is a religion of peace. In fact, I believe that if we as Muslims demonstrated grace and patience in the face of imagined, or actual, slights then we are likely to defuse the animosity that others may have toward us.

If there is animosity toward the idea of Islam or Muslims, then we should remember that there is more than one way of dealing with it. We can individually, and communally, demonstrate through our behavior that we carry no ill will to others. We can engage with Muslims and non-Muslims in the same manner. We demonstrate peace by refusing categorically to consider anger or violence as a response in our interactions with others.

My dream is to see a deep consistency in our behavior toward ourselves as Muslims as well as toward non-Muslims. For when we say that Islam is a religion of peace, we are making a tremendous statement. The idea of peace is not something that is divisible in my view. Peace is something that should not be offered when it is to our advantage and withdrawn when it is a burden. Peace is a state of being. Peace is a permanent stance toward the world. Peace makes real sense when it is offered as a response to anger, aggression, and violence. This is the peace that I see within Islam. When you hear the statement "Islam is a religion of peace" I want you to grab hold of the responsibility of peace. I want you to see this not as a defensive statement, but as a reminder of a great responsibility that you have toward Allah, toward others, and toward yourself.

CRISIS OF AUTHORITY

Saif,

There is a growing sense of responsibility within certain sectors of the Arab world for the spread of extremist thinking. Traditional so-called quietist scholars are connecting with one another and trying to frame principles and statements that will take control of the deteriorating public discourse within Islam. They are taking on the rebel and, often, terrorist Islamist opinion-formers and spokespeople. You need to be aware of the parameters of these debates, the passion and knowledge that are used in presenting positions as well as some of the spaces where you, as a thinking, ethical person, have the absolute right to intervene and judge the direction of the discussion. What are some of the parameters that I am referring to? A lot of debate revolves around the idea of defending the global Islamic community—the Ummah—and it is very difficult to move beyond the assumption that it is under attack. If you question this, you will find that you are going against the community. If you go further, and ask who defines the Ummah and what its interests are, you will find yourself in more hot water. These are not questions that are asked. Certainly not in public. And I wonder if they are ever asked in private. I certainly have not heard this type of question.

What other type of question is off-limits in mainstream, and powerful, Islam? The question of working and studying in a mixed-sex environment is a very sensitive subject. In strict Islamic societies, the mixing of the sexes in schools, universities, and in the workplace is frowned upon and sometimes legislated against.

What happens when you question the logic or the religiosity of such a position? You will be shouted down by the louder, more vociferous clerics. They will accuse you of wanting to promote immorality (unlawful sex) and fitna—social chaos. They will question your intentions and accuse you of a great crime against the stability of society.

Traditional scholars and rebel Islamist leaders of the day are at odds, each questioning the other's authority. In a strange turn of events, by openly practicing debate, they have actually created a new space for us lay Muslims to place a claim of some authority in the creation of new avenues for Islamic discourse. This crisis of authority might provide those of us who cannot claim power in a traditional sense an opportunity to channel the direction of Islamic discourse and debate conceptually, ethically, and philosophically during this time of great change. This can be done in so many ways. The most important ways are going to be through the written word, and through visual media. Why is the written word important? In a world of tweets, attention spans are shortening and people are thinking in little bites. But what are the masters of extremist Islam doing? They are building castles out of words. They are engaging in long legalistic arguments on the precise value of different actions. They are focusing on developing an advanced theology of death, destruction, and decay. If we are to work on combating this type of distortion of Islam, then we need to spend the time also working out in words, both spoken and written, the philosophical and theological arguments for a wholesome Islam. We need to fill the world of Islam with works of literary fiction that allow us to empathize with one another, and give words to our feelings.

The visual is also important. By developing the visual arts in the Islamic world we foster a way that allows our youth to express themselves nonverbally. We also need to develop film, whereby we can enchant one another with stories that come from our rich Islamic, and human, imagination.

The harsh reality is that the more narrowly defined the scope of religious knowledge and expertise, and the more exclusively protected it is, then the less relevance it will have and the less potency it will have. There is more than enough space within these debates for a range of people to participate, from philosophers to psychologists, from literary theorists to writers of contemporary fiction, from disenchanted young men to fallen and condemned women. It is evident that in this sphere, we will progress far more rapidly if we include everyone in the dialogue.

In fact, you will understand that so many people can contribute to religious and ethical debate that you should be surprised when the ulema still insist that only they can participate in the discussion. Yet within the ulema is a quiet but growing number who recognize that they do not have all the answers. This group, which is still not interconnected, understands that Islam cannot be dominated by a narrow band of "experts" who are often enticed by personal power and enrichment. This group of ulema recognizes that for Islam to be healthy and wholesome in the twenty-first century, many more people will need to be involved in the process of rejuvenation. So I will look forward with you and your generation to an ulema for the twenty-first century— who are not afraid of questions about knowledge, sexuality, philosophy, and difference.

RESPONSIBILITY

Dear Saif,

How should you and I take responsibility for our lives as Muslims? Should we think of ourselves as Muslims and continue living as individuals who are just minding our own business? Surely the important thing is to be a good person, which is more than sufficient for living a life that is good. What connection could there be between us and those criminals who scare us just as much as they scare Westerners?

Why should we have to apologize for the crimes committed by lunatics who claim they are acting for Islam? Lots of our fellow Muslims have protested against such events and have publicly condemned the crimes committed as well as having said that these people are not true Muslims. If we took this approach, you and I would have a lot of company. I hear every day that "those people have nothing to do with Islam." I hear this statement and I sit back and think, What is wrong with it? It does not sound right. I wonder why people say it. It is certainly a convenient way of avoiding responsibility. If it has nothing to do with Islam, then we are free to continue our everyday lives. It is also an easy way of not thinking through some very difficult questions.

I look at the matter from a different perspective. Though I do not like what the terrorists do, I realize that according to the minimal entry requirements for Islam, they are Muslims. The requirements to be a Muslim are to believe that there is no God but Allah and that Mohammed is the Messenger of Allah. The terrorists certainly believe this. Key religious institutions in the Islamic world refuse to condemn these terrorists as non-Muslims.

But the leading institutions of Islam do go one step further. They condemn the actions of these terrorists. This is good. This provides some moral clarity. In the view of the establishment of Islam, though the terrorists are Muslim in terms of faith, they are condemned for their actions.

This allows us within the Islamic faith an opening for taking responsibility for what the extremists are doing. There are different types of responsibility though. I am not saying that you and I are to blame for what the terrorists are doing. But I am saying that we can take responsibility for demanding a different understanding of Islam. We can take responsibility for making clear, to Muslim and non-Muslim, that another reading of Islam is possible and necessary. And you and I, as well as our friends, need to act in such a way that we make clear how we understand Islam and its operation in our lives. I believe we owe that to all the innocent people, both Muslim and non-Muslim, who have suffered at the hands of our coreligionists in their misguided extremism.

Saif, I think you have noticed by now that I see the world through the prism of responsibility. I want you to experiment with the idea of responsibility and see where it might take you. You must explore this idea in your own mind, in your reading, and in your daily life.

This leads me back to the position of those who talk of True Islam. I, as a Muslim, want to take as much responsibility for the world around me as I can. Load me up with responsibility. I refuse to pass the blame for things to other people. I relish the responsibility for good and bad. Why would I want this, Saif? I want it because it means that I am using all of my capabilities— physical, mental, and moral—to make the world a place for us to be proud of. Many people run away from responsibility. I once heard a senior manager advising his staff: take credit, not responsibility. This is precisely the opposite of what I want you to do. I want you to take responsibility even if you do not take the credit at the end. You will know the truth behind the outcomes achieved.

When you do not take responsibility, the world spins out of control. Without responsibility, you are on the run, you hide, you lower your head.

What kind of responsibility do I mean? Lots of people speak about responsibility and then get on with their lives as though nothing has happened. Responsibility means looking out for the disadvantaged in your community. Look for them. They will not always be visible. Our societies tend to focus on the new, the clean, the young, the beautiful. Who wants to think about the ugliness and unhappiness in life? I want you to devote some of your time to helping those who are on the borders of society. Do you have any idea how many orphans there are in the Arab and Muslim worlds? If you don't, then go and find out. If the facts are not organized, then go out and organize them.

Ask yourself the question: If I don't do it, who will? If you find the answer is no one will do it, then do it yourself. Look around for those who cannot read or write. As I tell you repeatedly, the Arab world has a hundred million illiterate people. Go out and build a volunteer organization to teach them this most basic of skills. Responsibility is around every corner, under every stone, in every household. Do not sit around like so many people do complaining that there are no opportunities and nothing to do.

Take back the definition of responsibility from those who would claim that responsibility is demonstrated by declaring violent jihad, or by carrying out suicide bombings. These are not examples of responsibility but of despair and depression. Responsibilities should be identified, and targeted. Responsibility is not picking up a gun and heading out to kill in the name of religion, not knowing who one is killing or why killing is necessary. It is a mockery of Islam to think that we are serving our faith and fellow Muslims by engaging in violence. In discussions that I have had with various people who support the violent approach, I am always puzzled by the insistence that violence is necessary. I wonder what problem violence solves. In fact, it seems like people are convinced of the moral worth of violence without really thinking about it. It is as though someone has brainwashed them into believing the act of violence is good in itself.

What might you say to such people? How do you speak to them? I respond with questions. What is violence for? What purpose is served? What consequences does violence carry with itself? Why do these people reach for violence as if it were the only tool in the box? What problem are they trying to solve?

Are there not a million more creative and interesting ways to solve problems? The reality is that violence is the tool of the unthinking. The resort to violence is a particularly unintelligent and unimaginative way to deal with matters. We should challenge ourselves to imagine ways in which we can solve problems and improve the situation of Muslims in the world through means other than violence. Ultimately, even those who think that violence is serving some purpose need to look at the effects of violence and realize that it only destroys.

Do you need more ideas? Look around yourself. Who looks like he or she is fearful or hungry, weak or humbled by life? Find out what they do. Understand whether they represent a unique case, or if they represent a class of people. If they are a solitary case, see how you can help them. If they represent a class of people, think about what system you can design to address their problem.

If you want to take responsibility, use what you have to support artists, writers, thinkers, filmmakers. Go out and be an artist, writer, thinker, or filmmaker. The Muslim world needs to reflect upon itself. The way for us to take responsibility is to go out into the world and do, take action, make the first move forward.

When you bear responsibility you raise your head, your mind is focused, and you sense a certain kind of dignity—the dignity that you should feel as a complete human being.

I want you to notice that there are at least two kinds of responsibility that I am referring to here. The first kind of responsibility is the responsibility you take for your own actions. And to take responsibility for your own actions, I believe you must first take responsibility for your own beliefs. This is the second type of responsibility.

This is a big demand. It is not easy to look at your beliefs and think through them. I believe you can do it. It is difficult, as words and ideas are slippery and can easily slide out of your control. This is why a lifelong search for knowledge through order and meaning are vital.

You may be certain of your beliefs about something today, only to wake up tomorrow wondering what it was that you believed in the first place. To admit this in today's environment is risky. Few people admit to having doubts about their own beliefs. Trust me, it is entirely normal to wonder if you got it right—about anything, let alone religious matters.

Sometimes our beliefs are dealt a blow by a personal tragedy, or by a catastrophic and incomprehensible event. We wonder what it is all for, or what it is all about. Some of the greatest scholars of Islam, highly respected today, went through periods of confusion and doubt. Al-Ghazali is an example. He was born in the eleventh century in Persia and has been hugely influential in Islamic thought. His works are treasured today as pearls of wisdom. But he withdrew from society for a decade because he was doubtful about many things. He seemed to have experienced a spiritual crisis. We may not know much about the doubts he had, but the fact that he was unsure and even fearful is clear. The outcome of his period of doubt and self-imposed isolation was that this scholar of Orthodox Islam brought the spiritual strain of Islam—Sufism—into the mainstream. His personal scholarship and ability to organize ideas intellectually allowed for the acceptance of ideas outside of strict orthodoxy. He opened up our religious experience to the spiritual and the poetic.

Anyone who has spent time learning and thinking will recognize the feeling of the confusion that new information and new ideas cause to previously held beliefs. This is also a normal reaction. When we come across new information and ideas, previous understandings need to be refined in order to accommodate the new input. The same processes happen in our religious and emotional lives. As we build up personal experiences with the world around us, we find that the clarities of childhood no longer ring true. They don't make sense. They seem too simple for a complex world. What presented itself as either black or white now contains many shades of gray. Black is not so black anymore, and white not so white. What do we do? Do we force ourselves to cling to earlier understandings that don't fit the world around us? Well, some people insist that this is the only way. Some people insist that they force themselves back into the box of an earlier consciousness. It is a futile task. Life is to be embraced as it is today. Knowledge cannot be evaded. Concepts and ideas exist in the air around us. We cannot choose to un-know ideas that came from somewhere else.

Some of our fellow Muslims insist that this is not only possible but also necessary. They demand that we accept only ideas that are Muslim in origin. This can include ideas that appear in the Quran, the early dictionaries of the Arabic language, and the sayings of the Prophet, and the biographies of the Prophet and his Companions. Foreign ideas are to be rejected as outside of the faith.

What are some of these ideas that we are told are foreign, and even alien, to Islam?

There is much discussion about whether democracy is compatible with Islam. Some say that discussion, debate, and consensus building are an ancient Islamic tradition. Others say that democracy is a sin against Allah's power, against his will, and against his sovereignty. People kill one another over this question. People radicalize and go underground to fight for Allah's sovereignty.

Another question revolves around the word *freedom*.

As I have told you elsewhere, freedom can mean freedom from the moral law, freedom to live what some Muslims regard as an animalistic life of pleasure without constraint. On the other hand, freedom can mean responsibility and the conscious choice to live a disciplined and principled life.

There is the broader idea that the Muslim and the Arab worlds are under attack by an Islam-hating West. This attack is said to take many forms, but the central one is the cultural invasion that threatens to undermine our identity and values. We watch movies in which women run away from home and live independent lives. We hear of artists' exhibits that are entirely blasphemous. These types of experiences open the minds of our youth to ideas that are alien to our culture. What would happen if our youth are no longer able to separate themselves from these foreign ideas and concepts?

The question of sexual identity and practice is becoming a topic that raises its head more frequently. The strict Islamic approach as interpreted today states that homosexuality is a choice and a sin. This is seen as a foreign idea being imposed by liberal, godless, Western states on the Islamic world in the guise of human rights. But what if we were to consider the idea that homosexuality is not chosen but genetically predetermined?

What about the idea of democracy? Is it really something that is completely alien to the Muslim mind?

What should we make of the radicals and the terrorists who claim that democracy takes away from Allah's power and sovereignty over mankind? Does what they say make any sense? Do these people even know what democracy is? I do not think they do. In fact, from reading many of their statements, it is clear that they have little understanding of how people can come together to make communal decisions. They also have no idea of how group decisions and morality interact. If you and I are to do justice to our faith, it is important to make the effort to understand how these ideas form, and how they can interact. It is also important to share this thinking with those around us. Those who act out of ignorance, and with violence, cannot be allowed to represent our faith.

There are a number of problems here that you should be aware of and for which I want you to try to develop your own answers. Do we really understand these foreign ideas? Do we know their history and origins, and the circumstances that gave them meaning? Must all foreign ideas be removed, even if beneficial? And really importantly, what should we do when an allegedly Islamic idea is clearly nonsense?

Another example of an idea that causes a great deal of concern to Muslims and non-Muslims alike is the mixing of the sexes. Some Muslim countries legislate separation of the sexes in schools, universities, and the workplace.

This approach is presented as being truly Islamic. What problems does this approach solve? It is argued that it solves the problem of illicit meetings and relationships outside of marriage. Perhaps it does. But research and study may show that it does not. We will not know until we ask the question.

Alongside this question, we need to also ask what problems does the separation of the sexes give rise to? We do not often talk about the problems that a supposedly moral approach can cause. It is time we started asking this question. Could it be that the separation of the sexes leads to psychological confusion and turmoil? Could it lead to an inability to understand the opposite sex when finally allowed to interact? Could it not perhaps be inconsistent with the mingling of the sexes in the marketplace or shopping malls, or when on holiday?

The broader question here is how should we deal with the many small "moral" steps that when added up together lead to an unhealthy and even possibly sick society. We need to take responsibility for these questions not only by asking them in public but also by responding to the possible answers to these questions. We all need to think whether we are missing the big picture as we try to lead an ethical life. These are all questions for you and your generation to think about.

Even more radical positions are taken by some people, who say that any idea uttered by a non-Muslim should be rejected. This can be expanded to include clothing—so some people will say that we must not copy the non-Muslim in his or her dress. This serves to confirm that Muslims are different from non-Muslims. But it also acts negatively to narrow the world in which we Muslims live. It stops the healthy and free flow of ideas that is so vital to mental health and intellectual vibrancy.

So there are leading Muslim figures who insist on rejecting the non-Muslim worlds of cultures and ideas. Well, they can insist on this, but it is insisting on the impossible. We need to look at the world of ideas as products of our common humanity. The task that we should set ourselves is to grasp these ideas, foreign or not, subversive or not, and to consider them within the principles of our faith. In this way rather than shunning responsibility and trying to hide our heads in the sand, we take responsibility for our ideas, and their evolution. We incorporate that which can be incorporated into our worldview. We absorb ideas and information and thereby take responsibility for deepening and enriching not only our self-understanding but also our understanding of our faith.

Once you accept responsibility for your beliefs, responsibility for your actions follows smoothly.

But what about the actions of others? What about those people who commit crimes in the name of Islam?

As I have said, many of our fellow Muslims say, it has nothing to do with us, it has nothing to do with Islam!

They are correct in a sense. They cling to a pure idea of Islam. What worries me is that as the ideas of these radical and extremist groups spread as potentially Islamic, the circle of Muslims clinging to another kind of Islam begins to shrink. And as it shrinks, it becomes quieter and quieter until only the extremists seem to speak and act in the name of Islam.

I worry about this. I worry for myself, and for you. I worry for our community. That is why I believe that it is not good enough to deny that the extremists have anything to do with Islam. In fact, I see that they have everything to do with Islam and with certain tendencies within our faith. The battle within Islam, as exemplified in the previous sentences, is a battle between those who have a narrow view that they express through their own violent natures, and a broad and generous understanding of Islam that is retreating in the face of the violence.

Now is not the time for us to shirk responsibility. In fact, I believe that if I can effect some change, then I am responsible for not engaging in making that change. I see the world as one that we construct ourselves through our beliefs and our actions. I want you to see it through this lens. If we do not like what the extremists are doing, then we need to call them out on it. It is too easy to say that they have nothing to do with us. They speak in Allah's name. And they do so convincingly. Even if their reading seems warped and out-of-date, it is a reading. It is a reading that has traction, that has popularity. We must react in some way. We must take action.

It is also not enough to chant in public that Islam is not violent or radical or angry—that Islam is a religion of peace. We need to take responsibility for the Islam of peace. We need to demonstrate how it is expressed in our lives and the lives of those in our community.

THE PERSPECTIVE OF
AN OUTSIDER

Habeebie Saif,

In this letter I want to talk to you about the idea of belonging to a group and what this can entail. Every person deals with this question at some stage of their lives. Some people are lucky enough to be born into a family where all the boxes are ticked. The father has power and recognition in his society or his religious or ethnic group, his wife comes from a well-established family, and his children enjoy the sense of belonging to a group that knows what it stands for. You can think of dozens of examples. You will know kids at school who carry the confidence of complexion, lineage, wealth, and connections. Some of them will be able to point to illustrious ancestors. Others will know all the right things to say and when to say them. Sometimes you will wonder whether what is right is determined by who is saying it. These kids can often be the "in" crowd at school.

Out in the workplace, you may come across many similar examples. Some people will get the best jobs and the best opportunities because of what group they belong to, not because of what they know. If you belong to one of these groups, you may even thank your lucky stars.

What happens if you are not a member of one of these groups? What if you see yourself as an outsider from the mainstream groups that populate society? What if, no matter what you try to do, you will always look and sound different?

Some of our fellow Muslims look at the world through this lens. Both in Muslim majority countries as well as in those countries where we are in the minority. Some of our truly deprived brethren, who do not know how to make a life for themselves in society, turn inward. They isolate themselves and look to those who can confirm their self-righteous anger and disappointment with what life has given them. The justifications are multiple. They can claim that they were condemned from birth because they are Muslim, or Arab, or curly haired, or brown. They can claim that they are condemned because they speak the local language with an accent. They can claim they are condemned because they are poor and will remain poor and cut off from economic opportunity because of subtly racist government policies.

All of these points may well be true. In fact, I have no doubt they are true, because I have experienced many of these forms of condemnation.

I know that you, Saif, have also experienced some of these things. I know that when you were at home you were discriminated against for being of mixed race. I know that you were criticized for being from a privileged family and class. I also know that you will be criticized in the future for having received an excellent education, as well as be criticized and feared for being an Arab and a Muslim.

So what do you do with these different forms of discrimination? Well, the most important idea I want to convey to you at this stage is that you should consider yourself burdened with privilege. Not because of what I do, or what I have given you. I want you to consider yourself privileged because you are alive, full of life, and because you have the opportunity to contribute something positive to this world. The negative comments, the overt racism, the negativity that can come from others because you or your group do not fit in with the dominant group—all this provides you with a richer perspective on social and economic justice. These negative attacks or comments give you the content for deeper reflections on what people's lives can and should be about.

I recognize that Islamophobia, or anti-Muslim sentiment, is a real and occasionally dangerous social manifestation. And I do believe that it is unbecoming of those who are Islamophobic. But do I believe that it gives us Muslims a way out of taking responsibility for our lives, and the life of the community? Not at all. Do I believe that Islamophobia is an irrational and incomprehensible phenomenon? Not at all. Do I believe that those who despise or mistrust Muslims are eternally held in the embrace of Islamophobia? Not at all.

All of this reality can be changed. It is up to you and I and others like us to make this change happen. Remember, though it is possible to demand change, it is better to effect change through your behavior, through your statements, through your consistency, through your advocacy. And if you stand up and demonstrate that you, in your so-called state of imperfection, can do better than any of your peers, then you will have gone a long way toward changing the perceptions that surround us. That's what I want you and your friends to do.

For many years, Saif, particularly when I was around your age, I tried hard to make myself fit in. I thought I could fit in by virtue of my effort and a bit of blindness. My main weakness in trying to fit into the Arab society I was born into was, and is, the fact that your grandmother is Russian.

Why would this be a problem? Well, like in any other

society, there are the original or privileged inhabitants, and then there are the newcomers, the upstarts, the half-castes, and the strays. Don't ask me why societies organize themselves this way. I don't know. But you will see it across the globe. I have seen it in Russia, France, and the UK. Some will point to a similar situation in the United States as well.

Having a Russian mother has colored my blood. It meant that others who could claim a "pure" bloodline could look down on me and my siblings. Guess what? They did. Repeatedly. I initially did not understand. I would argue with them and state that a family's standing in society was determined only by the father and that the mother had nothing to do with it. As time went by, I realized both that this was not how society operated as well as that I was negating my mother's existence. I was burying my head in the sand. You need to know that racism is not something invented in the West, or only experienced there. Racism exists in all societies. It is a reaction to people who do not fit the dominant mold of what people should be or look like. I do not want to compare what I experienced to racism of a greater order such as the experience of African Americans, or the Jews in Nazi Germany. The racism I experienced was much gentler, much subtler. It certainly was not violent or aggressive. But it was enough to make me think about how we deal with people who are different from ourselves. Given that I could not be considered a pure Arab, I realized that I was to be defined by being an outsider of sorts. This has proved to be a blessing and an advantage in so many ways. Being an outsider is humbling. It makes you realize the humanity of all outsiders. It opens up a great space of empathy between yourself and everyone else who looks like they are excluded from the group. This is a set of people rich in perspectives and experiences. It is often the outsider who has the most interesting view of what life is and can become.

To make matters worse, my knowledge of Arabic was next to nonexistent. Since my father had died when I was six and my mother spoke to us in Russian, my siblings and I came to see Arabic as a difficult and foreign language. This made my attempts to fit in an impossibility. Remember that we were growing up in a home where Arabic was not spoken. We spoke broken Russian with our mother, and English with one another, as a result of our schooling. An additional factor that influenced our language development was that the country was welcoming foreign experts from around the world in order to develop its basic infrastructure in the early 1970s. English became the common language among all communities. Today the problem of language has become more complex, not only because of the continued presence of a great number of foreigners, but also because of the spread of English as a global language of culture and knowledge. More and more Arab children are speaking and thinking in English as a first language, relegating Arabic to routine tasks and instructions in the home.

I came to a depressing conclusion at the age of fourteen. I realized that I was an outsider from all the things I wanted to be inside. I could not be the Arab I wanted to be. I could not be the Muslim I wanted to be. I could not rationalize my mother's foreign nature within the fixed ideas of belonging that I had. In reality, my siblings and I found ourselves caught between not only having both Arab and Russian blood but also speaking English as a first language because we attended English-language schools.

Saif, it is because I have lived my life as a half-race Arab who spoke Arabic with difficulty and had no father to rely on that I became aware of the importance of language, blood, and patriarchs. My youth was filled with attempts to fit in as a true-blood. I discovered that no matter how much you want to be a true-blood, and how much you defend the position of the true Arab or Muslim, if you aren't one, you cannot become one.

As I reflected upon my inability to be "true," it became imperative to discover other ways of justifying my existence to myself. And interestingly, in discovering the value of myself as a human being and a marginal one at that, I made one of the most important realizations an individual can make: it is as individuals that we have value, it is as individuals that we contribute and build, it is as individuals that we take responsibility and create new worlds, it is as individuals that we lay down in the earth at the end of our lives—as your grandfather did. There is no group to hold on to, there is no community that will protect you from incapacitating hardships, and there is no state that will share your pride in having carried out your responsibilities. The ultimate truth is that we are individuals who can choose to respect ourselves, and others, with or without regard to bloodline, wealth, tribe, or community.

However, dealing with the problem of authenticity as a personal matter was challenging because it required me to respond to this rejection, which ultimately constructed my understanding of being an individual— an Arab, a Muslim, and a person with dignity.

How did I respond to the fact that I could never be seen as authentic? There were two accessible response options, although the second option only became clear to me in my late thirties after a good dose of Nietzsche.

The first option was to recognize rejection—and follow its consequences. One of the truths I discovered many years later is that even if the group rejects you, this does not necessarily mean that you are not part of the group. The group develops and expands and grows in value by individual maturation and social interactions. My initial reaction was to absorb the rejection and wonder where I fit in. The framing of the problem in this way was logical for a young teenager and reflected the typical human desire to belong. I arranged with my mother for me to be sent to boarding school in England at the age of fifteen. This trajectory was a respite from the very trying period of rejection I experienced back at home. Boarding school was a mix of ethnicities and nationalities. Of course, there were questions of inclusion and exclusion from groups, but these groupings were not important to me then. I went to boarding school as an outsider by any classification, and it was in the outsider position that I felt able to rest and think.

The second option, as I said, came to me much later in life while reading various philosophical texts. I decided to impose myself as the standard and measure others by it. I decided to stop accepting others as role models. I decided to fashion myself, knowing that I could never be 100 percent genetically Arab. I stopped accepting the low and sometimes impossible standards of others around me, since I was too different for their standards to make any sense in my life as an individual with dignity. This is a more complex way of saying that I decided to be myself. This is perhaps the challenge that I believe young Arabs and Muslims face without realizing it. There are powerful political forces and social mechanisms that operate to impose very strict and one-dimensional standards for what it is to be a person in our particular philosophical universe. Such standards display a misreading of how the modern world operates. Each of us has a name and a face and a set of dreams, wishes, and desires. Each of us has his own set of motivations and sources of pride. Not allowing for these dreams and motivations and desires to be translated into political mechanisms that afford them the chance to be realized is ultimately catastrophic. There is no such thing as al Sha'ab—the People. This word refers to a time when we were faceless crowds with no power over our own lives. Each of us is an individual who now has the technological means of discovering himself or herself by witnessing what the rest of the world is doing.

There is a growing sense of acceptance for the individual in parts of the Arab world primarily as a result of social media and information through the Internet. A specific illustration is the mirrorlike function of having a Facebook page. Facebook operates in several ways—as a platform to allow for individual expression as well as to undermine the powerful mechanisms traditionally operating on our youth. It creates a space for the individual to look at his or her page as an expression of themselves. The paucity of photographs or videos and links on one's page is a reflection, in a way, of the emptiness or fullness of that person's life. There is a compulsion set in motion to fill the space with yourself. This is then compounded by the ability to attract friends to look at your page and provide commentary on your content. And last, it provides you the autonomy to determine your accessibility or your privacy, to limit or expand audiences, to be how you want to be without fear of repercussions. These are powerful mechanisms within the reach of any child in the Arab and Muslim worlds and therefore are to be regarded as a vital antidote to the manipulative and fundamentalist mechanisms devouring our youth.

Growing up, before Facebook, the advice I would often hear was to "be yourself." This advice is powerful but empty at the same time. Had I known what "myself" was, it would have been easier to be it. The advice may be better expressed: find yourself, look for yourself, discover yourself, shape yourself, fill the gaps of yourself, draw clearer lines around the areas of yourself that you recognize, discipline yourself, and test yourself.

Every young Muslim should demand his or her right to discover the world and himself or herself, using the tools of self-knowledge and self-mastery.

I would hope that it becomes clear that the ownership of one's self in today's world means that you engage with today's world. The dominant narratives demand that we reject today's world (as if it can be rejected) and embrace an ancient world that exists mostly in our imagination. We are led to read select texts that are presented in a language far from the language that we use in our daily lives. You know that there is a significant difference between what is known as Classical Arabic, based on the language of the Quran, and the dialects of spoken Arabic, which differ greatly from one to the other.

True, these texts form a core part of our history, but it is an untreated history, an unquestioned history, an unexplored history, and, very likely, an incomplete history. In a sense, it is like asking Londoners to live like the class of barons under King Henry VIII—and only like that class.

Even if the idea of living according to the standards of sixteenth-century court politics is acceptable, we need to remember there were many other types of living at that time. Not everyone was a baron, just as not everyone in our distant past was a warrior for Islam. There were all types of people who performed all sorts of functions. Discounting such elements of our history will distort reality and impede individuals from taking the paths appropriate to their own circumstances.

This is a major problem for you and your generation. It makes it difficult to think of being a Muslim with your own identity, your own personality and preferences. It makes it easier for others to tell you that you do not have a right to be an individual who is special in his or her own right. The stories you are exposed to give you the impression that the only way you can be a proper Muslim, in accordance with the Quran and the Prophet's example, is if you behave the way people did in the seventh, eighth, and ninth centuries.

And of these models, the most prominent and politically useful are the models of ancient heroism and bravery in the face of unimaginable odds. You and your generation run the risk of being deprived of any understanding of the pride of perseverance in work, responsibility, learning, and family. You and your generation are tempted with power and adrenaline—and a paper-thin life on the margins of a marginal part of the world, with the promise of the afterlife.

Yet what I have told you only concerns the easy parts of being different—the stuff that concerns your DNA, your bloodline, your lineage, and your ethnicity. Things get even more interesting when we begin to think about the world of ideas.

Being part of the group entails also having a set of ideas that can identify you as a group. Within the Muslim communities of the Arab world, there seems to be a tendency to coalesce around certain clear ideas. These ideas concern not only Islamic doctrine—that once decided cannot be thought about or challenged— but also behavioral aspects that identify the sect to which you belong. The set of ideas can go further into what seems superficial but can have profound effects, such as not mixing with non-Muslims, or trying to import Western technologies but not Western culture or ideas.

This is the attempt to maintain Islamic purity as defined by the elite of the particular group. But is it possible to maintain this type of purity in the modern world of social media and the globalized economy? I want you to think about this question not just from the perspective of a young Arab and Muslim, but also from the perspective of all those who would presume that they are different and superior in other societies.

PATH TO FUNDAMENTALISM

Habeebie Saif,

I remember how easy it was to find a religious path when I was a boy. I was twelve and had just spent a summer month in a school to memorize the Quran. My Arabic was very poor at the time and I was not used to memorizing reams of information the way they did in Arabic-language schools. I was out of my element. I felt very lonely.

As the weeks progressed, I became mesmerized by the sounds of the recital. In other letters I talk about this at length. The summer was intense. There were no air conditioners in the rooms, and the door would be left open to allow in the air. Outside it often reached over 115 degrees Fahrenheit. Lessons would start at 7 A.M. and go on until 1 P.M.

The lessons consisted of reciting lengthy passages of the Quran. Each student took turns facing the teacher and reciting. This could often be a comic affair as the lazier students attempted to cheat with open Qurans lying about or by having a friend whisper forgotten words to prompt another memorized verse. Once this was accomplished, the lesson would move on to reading a new passage of the Quran, listening to an explanation of it, and agreeing on the new passages to be memorized for the next day. If I remember correctly, the daily amount to be memorized came up to three pages, or forty-five lines. An astounding number for me to consider even today. There was certainly a lot of mental power and stamina in that classroom.

My older brother, Adnan, was also in the class with me. I really cannot remember much of the hours we spent there. I only remember meeting my brother in the car that would take us to the school. Then he would disappear somewhere in the class. Some other memories pop up. The sound of the Quran being recited by some of the less diligent students. This was to hear the Quran in a lesser form. It sounded less holy. Or perhaps it was holy but not smooth and flowing the way we all knew that it should have been if properly recited.

And then there was a young boy who always made me think of my father. He was shorter than most of the boys in the class. He held himself straight and you could feel his energy and focus. I was somewhat envious. He was miles ahead of all the other students. I remember hearing him recite three pages without a single fault, with not a second's hesitation. It was as though he were reading the text directly from the book. I witnessed him doing this every day for the month we were at the school. I would wonder why I could hardly memorize three to four lines a day, whereas he could completely absorb and become the words of the Quran.

Knowing that the Quran is the word of Allah, I envied his ability to become the voice of Allah, metaphorically of course.

The month passed and I had clearly been soaked in a religious environment that I still wonder about today. I was glad that I was out, since I could spend the rest of the summer sleeping in.

Years later I realized how deeply this short period at Quran school affected me. Both positively and negatively. Saif, as I write the word *negatively* I smile with a touch of nervousness. It sounds wrong to say that there could have been anything negative about a period dedicated to learning the Quran. Many people you and I know would react with horror at the thought. But what if it really is the case that there were some negative consequences to this intense period of Quran immersion? What is the point of denying it? Reality denied sets us all back further. So I do not deny the negative. Just as I welcome the positive.

When I left the school with my brother, we were all

given a small sum of money as a reward from the government for having spent the month at the school. But at the last minute, the school deducted 20 percent for the Palestinian cause. This made a few of us feel cheated out of our "wages." Surely it would have been fairer to give us the option to donate the money. In any case, the point was made. The connection between religion, money, and politics was created in my mind. I spent little time thinking about the events of the month and looked forward to an easy four weeks at the home of my cousin.

My older brother and I were carted off to my older cousin's home, where we were given a beautiful and luxurious room to share. Evenings were spent drinking tea after dinner, in front of the TV coverage of the brutal war of 1982 when the Israelis invaded Lebanon. Arab TV stations did not hide any of the gory details. The images of maimed or dead young children will forever be etched in my mind. I can see the images now as I type these words.

At my cousin's house that summer, I was introduced to our new Arabic-language teacher one morning. I liked him. He was young and energetic and he had a ready laugh. I still see him these days. He is the same wonderful person I knew then, except for a distinct change in his political views. He is calmer and more accepting of the injustices in our world than he was then.

In the afternoons, I found myself reaching for the Quran and trying to memorize passages. I remember I would lock myself in one of the bedrooms and read passages out loud, imagining that I was one of the master reciters. Now I realize that there are rules to recital that take time to learn. So it means that I was just shouting out the verses in a singsong manner that would have sounded uneducated to anyone listening.

The Quran recital attempts melded with the TV images and the Arabic lessons over the course of those four weeks at my cousin's. Now I look back and realize that the combination of these influences was having a powerful effect on me. My world had been redirected along a path parallel to what I had been used to at my normal day school.

My Arabic teacher was very cautious with me when I began to talk to him about the things I had seen. There were times when he would smile and tell me I was too young to be talking about such matters as justice and revenge. There was more than enough time to talk about these matters later. Then, on occasion, as though letting me into a secret, he would agree with me that revenge was necessary and that one day we would be in charge. No one would be able to humiliate us.

We began to read short histories of the early battles of Islam. He made the words on the page come to life, and

I felt that I was there, a warrior in an ancient battle. And it felt right and correct.

He quickly became my source of knowledge regarding the revolutionary potential of Islam. Islam was now linked in my mind not just to piety, prayer, and the promise of a pleasurable afterlife, but also to questions of justice and politics and power and the right to control others. This was clear to me at the age of twelve, since if we were the ones who were striving continually to be morally correct, and morally informed, then surely we were the ones who had the right to decide how society should be directed. Furthermore, we were genuinely concerned with the grand questions of fighting injustice and protecting our fellow Arabs and Muslims wherever they were. These noble impulses were sufficient to give us the confidence that we had the right to decide for all others. Certainly we had more right than those who were concerned with money and pleasure and triviality like the comforts of daily life. I see similar positions being taken by Islamists and radical Muslims today.

I remember how I felt at the time. I was part of a revolutionary religious impulse that had certainty about all aspects of life in this world, coupled with the absolute exhilaration of the rewards of the afterlife. So why do I write about it in a way that suggests I am not an enthusiast of this way of life?

Today, I still meet many people who utilize the same approach, based on the same impulses and convictions. They are integrated into society and the economy the way any other Muslim is. But I still feel that there is something missing and I think the answer lies in the absence of doubt. By doubt, I mean the broad sensation of humility in the face of a world that is continually changing and evolving; humility in the face of facts that appear in the media as though they were carved in stone only to be discarded in the next news cycle as irrelevant tripe. The speed with which the presentation of events mutates is one reason why I feel that the certainties of the Islamists are doomed.

Saif, our convictions are undermined by our evolving perceptions. This simply means that the rigidity of the worldview that we were taught as children loses its validity as we mature. That worldview is one that is open to evolution as we add more features to it. A concern for the question of justice and injustice is extremely important; yet acting as though this concern gives us precedence in society should be seen instead as a power-grabbing ruse. We need to be conscious of this undercurrent. The worldview that says I am being ethically correct if I follow all the rules is one that can evolve into something more systematic— and more responsive to a more complex and nuanced understanding of the world around us. We evolve from ascertaining the specific rigid rules to discerning the principles of behavior that stand behind, or underpin, these rules.

These are some of the ideas that I see could have helped me in the early 1980s. Had we been educated not just in the rules, but also in the values that supported these rules, we might have been slightly more at ease in a world of change. The reality is that today, the dominant voices of Islam are increasingly shrill in their insistence on rule-following as the path to salvation. Why should this be the case? Part of the answer lies in the disconnect of senior religious scholars from the concerns of nonscholars in the Islamic world. Part of the answer lies in the disdain with which we are treated by a global community of Islamic scholars who have, consciously or not, created a monopoly over religious knowledge and authority.

Saif, you and your generation need to look at the dangers that this monopoly of religious knowledge and dialogue creates, and at some of the incentives that we all have in wishing to see this monopoly evolved into a broader understanding of the parameters of relevant knowledge.

We need to find a theological and social space and place for the following ideas: doubt, question, inquiry, and curiosity.

In our current environment, any doubt about

canonical beliefs risks the doubter being condemned as blasphemous and could lead to various death sentence fatwas. These are social and institutional mechanisms to stop people of your generation from thinking clearly about your own lives. Our religious leadership needs to step up and speak to the issue of what we don't speak about in our societies. These are the unanswered questions of moral responsibility, meritocracy, and nepotism, of sexuality and our biological determinants, among other questions.

Saif, these are the questions of your generation. Don't let anyone tell you that a question buried is a question answered. This is the easy and foolish way out. It is impossible to ignore questions and think that we have thereby negated their existence. Too many times, the answer of our religious authorities is to say that even posing the question is wrong, incorrect, or immoral.

As you grow and meet more people outside of your immediate school environment, you will see a pattern that is repeated in our region, and perhaps in our Islamic faith, when a young man, generally speaking, finds religion. He then casts aside all his previous friends and associations. He gives himself with unyielding, steel-like zeal to a life of militant devotion. He is seeking moral perfection and incorruptibility, and his piety is theatrical. He claims to be concerned for the lost souls of his previous friends. A normal, sociable, outgoing person is transformed into a one-dimensional all-knowing, all-criticizing man of prayer. This phenomenon can last a relatively long time. Invariably there is a crack in the rock of conviction, and the young man finds himself not quite so ready to continue along his chosen path. And the same pious individual on some future day appears at a party, drunk and cavorting with prostitutes, declaring that his religiosity was a phase and he is a new man. There is mild embarrassment.

I have asked myself over the years whether this is my imagination or whether this phenomenon really does take place. I have countless friends who have passed through a similar process of extreme devotion and piety and then feel a sudden relaxation and uncertainty about the entire experience.

I also suffered from depression as a direct result of not having the answers to the contradictions I saw between belief and the world around me. It lasted three years before depression and loneliness finally gave way to tears and a complete inability to make sense of these differing worldviews. I had rejected friends with whom I had grown up. We had shared experiences and we once bonded as children. In a way, I understand now that we were actually vital to each other. To reject a friend with whom you have grown up is to reject a fundamental part of your own personality and history. We grow up in human interaction with one another. This was something that was implicitly rejected by the religious dogma propagated by word of mouth in the school corridors and the school mosque. I see this same rejection of the human, communal component in twenty-first-century dogmatic versions of Islam. I imagine that it can only lead to the same sense of emptiness and anxiety that I and others of my generation experienced.

In this letter I wanted to demonstrate to you the innocent and well-meaning path that any one of us can follow in the desire to be a good Muslim. Saif, I want you to be aware of the well-constructed path to a closed worldview that will, if followed, lead a person to a dangerous place. It can lead a well-meaning and sincere child to a place of close-minded anger and aggression. It is not inevitable, nor is it necessary. It is possible. How to guard against it? You guard against it by remembering that life is to be lived and that there is always more than one way of dealing with obstacles. I reached a place of isolation and anger, fueled by religious certainties. Today I realize that certainties are not a privilege and a blessing but an obligation and a burden. Certainty should be gentle and cautious, not aggressive and angry. I hope that you can learn from the well-trodden path I have described to you here and keep an eye out for where goodness really abides. Within you and your gentle certainties.

VIOLENCE

Habeebie Saif,

As much as I don't like the topic, I have to talk to you about violence, in religion and, more broadly, in life. The reality is that though we talk of one Islam, we express it in different ways. You have a choice to give priority to certain principles and certain values. If you choose to express Islam in a violent and destructive manner, this is your projection onto Islam, of your personality and your choices. The same applies if you decide that your approach to life is one of balance, of measure, and of cooperation. Islam has within it the resources for you to be a complete and balanced person. But if you pick at the pieces within the history and texts of our faith that appeal to an inner anger and frustration, then you will have to carry the burden of that choice.

There is violence everywhere. In every religion, including Islam. Our task is to understand the boundaries of violence. And measure the use of violence against the moral and ethical laws that govern us.

As you develop an approach to the world, to history, to texts, and to understanding what other people are demanding of you, you will need to ask yourself what violence is for, what it does, and what it expresses. If you begin to think about these questions, you will discover that you are ahead of many people much older and more experienced than you.

Saif, your grandfather's life ended in violence. The violence was instantaneous, unexpected, and utterly destructive. It was also pointless and futile. It achieved nothing. It sent ripples out through time all the way till today. It was a single moment of violence that echoes through the decades. Does its effect grow weaker? I do not think so. The violence that destroyed your grandfather in 1977 continues to warp relationships and emotions in our family today. The effects of that violence continue to motivate me and color my view of the world.

I remember I was twelve and reading the newspapers about his death.

Though the violence perpetrated against my father was not inspired by religion, the question of violence has been central in my life. The question of violence is going to be central in the lives of your generation of

Muslims as well. Why? The reason is the rising voices of aggressive clerics who portray Islam as a religion of power through violence. These clerics are projecting a worldview onto Islam that ties the experience of early Islamic empires to the core of our religion. In doing this, they have built a system of ideas and theories that insist Islam is a religion that must dominate religiously, territorially, and militarily.

The reasons behind their worldview are multiple. I see simplistic ideas of what the history of Islam is really about. I also see that these clerics lead strangely frustrated lives locked in a world of narrow hate and anger. This hatred, anger, and frustration is not intrinsic to Islam. It is intrinsic to the narrow lives that these people have chosen to lead. Otherwise, how is it possible that some of these clerics have spent decades theorizing and debating the exact, almost mathematical, conditions for waging violent jihad? What would make a person of sound mind dedicate their lives to developing theories on when it is religiously permissible, or obligatory, to go out and kill others?

Other reasons are institutional and bureaucratic. These clerics are part of systems of knowledge and learning. If they go against the dominant themes and tendencies, they risk not progressing within their institutions.

And importantly, they demonstrate a lack of knowledge of the possible ways in which a human being can live a worthy life, as well as a complete lack of imagination regarding the possibilities for Muslim flourishing.

My question to the clerics who are obsessed with the theology of violence and death: Where are your learned theories on the role of kindness and generosity? Why, if you can write hundreds of pages of text on the theology of death, can you not give equal attention to what we Muslims can do with life? Why the intense focus on departing this world in a storm of blood and anger?

These are some of my questions.

You and your generation live in a richer and more diverse world. The arguments around violence are now available to you in many forms. All you need to do is to open your eyes and ears and look around you. Whatever religiously inspired arguments set out before you and your generation, the overwhelming evidence demonstrates that violence serves almost no positive purpose. I see only the very subtle threats of violence that are used as deterrents to violent behavior as occasions of positive value.

Of all the types of violence that we may face in our daily lives, it is the invitation to participate in so-called religiously sanctioned violence that worries me most. Your generation has shown itself to be particularly susceptible to this invitation. It is an invitation proffered to the weak minded, and the weak willed. It is an invitation sent out to those who cannot conceive of more fulfilling ways of living and serving their faith.

The invitation to violence is offered like a drug might be, or alcohol. It is a short route to immediate empowerment and satisfaction. But it is as equally destructive as, if not more so than, alcohol or drugs. The ticket to violence is an adrenaline-filled high that allows the religiously inspired aggressor complete license and freedom from any moral rules. If you look at the behavior of jihadists engaged in violent acts, in most cases against innocents, you will discover that the rules of moral behavior do not apply to them all of a sudden. Why is this the case? It is comic, but the argument is that they are engaged in a greater cause and so can be excused the smaller moral errors they commit.

I want you to see how giving in to the human lust for easy empowerment and violence turns the moral world upside down. Once entered into, the world of violence has its own dynamics that have nothing to do with the supposed moral aims that we are trying to achieve. Violence is sold to us, by some from within our faith, as the noblest and most effective means by which we can defend our faith from attack.

It is a fiction that our faith is under attack. It is a

fiction that violence brings good things in its wake. And it is a fiction that violence is a noble and effective means to achieve anything other than itself.

The greatest crime that some of our clerics commit is to tempt our youth with the promise of heaven if they undertake a suicide mission. This insane idea, which unfortunately is presented as the greatest sacrifice that we can make, is misleading. It may be true that the greatest sacrifice that a person can make is to give his life for a cause. But it is not the most difficult sacrifice a person can make.

The more difficult and perhaps more valuable sacrifice a person can make is to face the complexity of modern life and live life to its fullest—morally, spiritually, and socially. It is far more difficult to deal with the troubles thrown up by a globalized economy, the complexities of modern city life, and the utter sense of futility that all of us feel at some stage. And morally far more important.

This is the true challenge of a religiously inspired life. Not to head for the quickest exit in a cloud of fire and smoke. The moral life is to be lived through thick or thin, in easy circumstances and the most difficult. In fact, the moral life makes most sense when we are faced with the challenges that threaten to tear apart our societies—poverty, anonymity, fear, hopelessness. This is when we are tested by our own beliefs and when we need to respond by affirming our commitment to building sense out of our circumstances.

This is how I want you to approach the question of violence and how to respond to those who might tempt you and your generation. I often wonder what we can do to stop the violence. I often wonder whether we differ from others when it comes to violence. If we are different, then it is only because we have become accustomed to accepting certain ways of talking to one another and describing the world. What do I mean? Well, much of the violence that we find in our Islamic texts comes from the writings of the fourteenth-century theologian Ibn Taymiyyah. His texts are full of references to the obligation to kill, execute, and respond with violence of some sort.

What we need to be aware of is that he was writing at a time when violence was inflicted on the Muslims of his era by the Mongols who had invaded Baghdad. This was a terrible violence in itself. Massacres took place at the hands of the Mongols, and the Islamic world trembled with fear.

Modern-day radical Islamists describe the challenges facing the Muslim world today in the same terms as the Mongol invasion. Could this be why the response is along the same lines as that proposed by Ibn Taymiyyah? But is the Islamic world under such a threat? I do not think so. And if the Islamic world were under such a threat, aren't there more productive and interesting ways to respond to the challenge?

We all need to evaluate what threatens us as Muslims, and what threatens our faith. I will tell you that the threats that we are warned against come from the fever-ridden imaginations of people who have not left their neighborhood. These are imagined threats and challenges. In fact, what they are doing is using the outsider, and the West, as a scapegoat for our own failings within Muslim societies. There is no one out there trying to keep us down in misery, ignorance, and poverty. If we are to be angry with anyone because of the deprived situation that many of our fellow Muslims live in, then we should turn that anger toward ourselves for not having been creative enough, and dedicated enough, in building our societies. Violence should be put behind us and never be presented as an option. Violence is the tool of the frustrated and the angry. It achieves nothing for us as Muslims.

ROLE MODELS

Habeebie Saif,

You will hear a lot of people talking and writing about the need for role models for young people to use as guides to living well. What you may not know is that behind the scenes, far away from the open discussion of role models, there are very powerful and ancient models at work.

In the case of our Islamic faith, there is an ongoing battle to keep certain role models in the forefront. These are specific people, starting with the Prophet Mohammed and his immediate Companions. Of course, you know that because of the disputes between the early Companions, the Sunni and the Shiites differ strongly over who can be regarded as a worthy role model. The Shia hold up the Prophet's cousin Ali bin Abi Talib as the role model worth emulating because of his widely recognized wisdom and closeness to the Prophet. The

Sunnis hold Ali to be a role model, but also include the Rightly Guided Caliphs Abu Bakr, Omar, and Othman. These three key Companions of the Prophet are openly reviled by some modern-day Shias because of their treatment of Ali. The disputes themselves are important to the development of the modern Muslim world. What is perhaps more important is how we deal with a historic dispute over power if we are concerned with ethics in the modern world. That's why I do not want to go into more detail about this ancient disagreement. I just wanted to point out that these individuals are seen today as role models to one or another Muslim group.

What happens when we take a step back and lower our sights? How reasonable is it to think that someone can model their life on the Prophet's life? It is not as easy as people might think. We certainly cannot follow the model of the Prophet by receiving a Message of our own from Allah, or by reenacting the first few years of Islam. The Prophet was special. He fulfilled a very important role as the Seal of the Prophets. That's it. No one can come along and model himself on the Prophet's mission.

The only way in which we are offered the Prophet as a role model is by following his daily behavior as it has been transmitted to us through the sayings of the Prophet. This is noble and worthy. But we come to a point where we need to make decisions.

There are many things the Prophet did not do or could not have done, and so we have glaring gaps when we try to follow him as a model. Hence, the famous statement of a leading Islamic theologian to the effect that he would not eat watermelon because he did not know how the Prophet had eaten it—since there was no hadith, or saying. This may or may not have been said, but it does point to a style of thinking that is common among certain groups of Muslims. The only way in which they can be true to the life of the Prophet as lived in his daily detail is by putting the clock back to the seventh century. This type of role-play is found in premodern societies.

This type of life is appealing. It presents a kind of Islamic return to nature. It is a return to the original state of Muslim society. Or at least an imagined state of Muslim society. The reality is that this type of model is built on texts and historical imagination. This model clashes with something in the twenty-first century.

I was going to say to you that it clashes with the twenty-first century and the modern world. I actually think it is more accurate to say that this model clashes with the possibilities of life in the twenty-first century and the modern world. This is perhaps the key weakness that we need to tackle. Do our Islamic role models lock us out of the modern world, or can they allow us into the modern world?

There is one unfortunate model that has survived through the centuries: the warrior. When I think back to the lessons we would receive in our Islamic history classes, I remember very clearly the lists of battles that we would have to memorize. These were the early battles fought by the Prophet and his Companions in the first few years of Islam. Battles with names like Uhud, and Yarmouk, and Badr. We would need to know where they took place, the numbers of soldiers on each side, the heroic and shrewd performance of the Muslims in defeating their enemies. At that time, there were periods when the Muslims were under attack or threatened with attack, and periods when they went on the offensive. Alongside these stories, we would be told stories of the heroism of the Prophet, and his Companions. These were men with names like Omar al Khattab, and Abu Bakr al Siddiq.

Of course, Abu Bakr and Omar followed later in the footsteps of the Prophet and both became rulers (caliphs) of the Muslims after his death. We were taught about the great warrior Khalid ibn al Walid who led the armies that conquered Palestine and Syria. His name is etched into my memory due to the countless number of times I have heard him being praised. In fact, I was in Moscow in early 2015, at a light lunch with two highly educated businessmen from the Caucasus whose faces lit up with pride when Khalid ibn al Walid's name and exploits were mentioned.

This is one instance of the practical and palpable resonance our ancient warriors have in the twenty-first century. Another warrior often mentioned is Tariq ibn Ziyad, who led the Muslim armies into the Iberian Peninsula. These names still have the power to move people today. These men are glorified and raised high above normal Arabs and Muslims as examples of what the Arab Muslim world is able to produce.

This history of armies of Muslims, and tremendous heroism against the odds, and the specific characteristics of the heroes of Islam are what I took from school. We never got any further than the first four rulers of the Muslim world after the Prophet. They are known today as the Rightly Guided Caliphs, as their rule is seen by the Sunnis as the best period of Islam. And it is to this period that we are always called to return by those with a fixation on the past.

If this period of our Islamic history is characterized by anything, it is that we were energized with youth, military skills, the power of success, and faith in Islam. It was a time of expanding borders and powerful warriors acquiring the spoils of war.

This was not a time of great administrators, or large bureaucracies, or peaceful relations with neighbors. It was not a time of steady growth or stability. In order to rise to the top, and acquire wealth and property, it was necessary to be a warrior and fight. This was also not a time for poets, builders, or philosophers. It was the time to create a place for Islam in a chaotic and violent world.

This is perhaps why so much of our focus in looking for role models in Islam is on the warrior type. This approach to our own history is going to have an effect on how you and your generation will interpret the world. This is what I think is happening. So many young men, and some women, think that the only way to be a hero is by following in the footsteps of the warriors of early Islam. This idea is exploited by the religious clerics and some self-declared scholars to drive young Muslims into the arms of recruiters for a pointless war in the deserts of the Arab world, the mountains of Asia, and the villages of Nigeria, Mali, and Cameroon. When we join the army in a modern Arab or Islamic country, are we thinking about soldiering in a seventh-century sense or one that is more in tune with modern requirements? Is it time to add more dimension both to our history of Arab-Islamic wars of conquest as well as our Arab-Islamic history conceived more broadly?

The modern manifestation of the warrior is not the army general in his barracks with his loyal troops, or a young Napoleon, but rather the solitary, lonely, obedient, "misfit" type of young man who ends up being a suicide bomber or jihadist in Afghanistan or Syria. There are endless numbers of videos on YouTube of young men making their final statements before heading off to certain death. They show a mixture of pride, simplicity, resignation, and determination. They intend to make the ultimate commitment a human can make to an idea: offering one's life as a sacrifice.

The warrior is one of the sadder figures in our modern Muslim society. Sad because he thinks that he is acting in a way that will bring him closer to Allah, and to the rewards of the afterlife when, in fact, it is really opting out of the challenges of the life that Allah gave him.

What I want you to remember, Saif, is that there are ancient models of behavior that are operating in the world today. It is up to you and your generation to identify these models and think about them. You need to judge whether they are of any relevance to the modern world.

The idea of the warrior is powerful. Perhaps your generation can rethink its power in a positive and productive way. Perhaps the modern Muslim warrior is one who embraces life in its complexity and fights for social and economic justice with his or her mind, rather than for a stretch of desert territory with his or her body. Perhaps by looking at why we still cherish the model of the warrior, we might begin to understand where we have fallen behind the rest of the world. You and your generation should ask why certain strains of modern Islam are providing the warrior ideal as a worthy and useful mode of life.

What you need to realize is that history through the eyes of warriors is only one part of history. If we looked further into our history, and looked at what came after the Rightly Guided Caliphs, we would find that things settled down. Cities like Damascus and Baghdad were built, dynasties were formed, the Muslims split into groups that fought sometimes for the truth, and sometimes for power. The history of this period is messier, less clear in its meaning, and perhaps even less noble than the time of the Prophet.

We as Muslims take pride in the succession of Islamic empires such as the Ummayad, the Abbasid, and the Fatimid empires. We take pride in the preservation of the texts of ancient Greek philosophy by the early Muslims. We take pride in the achievements of the scientists of medicine and mathematics of Islam such as Avicenna and Al Khawarizmi.

If we could accept the role models of this period, we would have a larger number of characters to choose from. This would include the builders, the thinkers, the philosophers, the medical pioneers, the mathematical geniuses, the comic poets, and the intellectual rebels. If you want to be true to your Muslim heritage, then you need to explore its history properly. You and your generation need to study it and realize that Islam was never a one-dimensional army of fanatical recruits for war, as we are told by those who seem to speak loudest. Islam was a vibrant, exciting, intellectually adventurous, and logically rigorous religion. It was a religion of life and growth. It was a religion of worship and the world.

I looked for real life role models and historical role models myself after my father's death and then into my teens and early twenties. Where were the behavioral tracks I could follow without having to reinvent the wheel? And if I was having difficulty orienting myself, then perhaps others were too.

By the time I was eleven, the Lebanese Civil War had been raging for six years. The civil war in Lebanon arose out of the great mix of religions, sects, and ethnicities in that region. Carefully balanced relations were torn apart by the changing sizes and needs of the different communities. The presence of Palestinian refugees added to the growing pressures on the state until it was no longer possible to keep the peace. Different religious and ethnic groups began to arm themselves and form militias for self-protection. The situation rapidly deteriorated.

At school, we were beginning to hear about various

groups and different areas of Beirut. Occasionally Lebanese classmates would get into arguments about their respective positions on the civil war, depending on which militia they, or their parents, were aligned with. These hints of organized political violence were beginning to seep through to the classroom. The complication of the role of the Palestinians—as outsiders to Lebanon, and as Muslims—meant that there was an almost incomprehensible soup of militias with shifting loyalties and incredibly brutal tactics.

I remember this as the start for me personally of the idea of Arab men, and the occasional woman, being glorified as fighters of incredible bravery or ingenuity or sacrifice. Names would be thrown around, but more often it was simply a description—a twenty-three-year-old man or a sixteen-year-old girl had done something or other that would be praised. Some of us would mull over these acts of heroism and imagine taking part in these part-make-believe, part-real stories.

Everyone seemed to have had a cousin who had died in the fighting. Always an innocent, always so beautiful or handsome. Always so clever and with so much to live for. That's why revenge was vital, this is why the war was necessary, to rid the family or the group of the shame of one of their own being killed by the others.

Alongside these stories of individual bravery and sacrifice, we became more acquainted with the group mentality supported at the school mosque, as well as the rhetoric of unity and dignity that we were all inculcated with. In and of themselves, these elements of our history and culture and religion are valuable. But I observe, at a distance of over thirty years, the negative and limiting nature of the mix of elements that was propagated in our education and the media at the time.

Many nations inculcate specific values through the teaching of their history in schools. I have thought regularly about the specific values we were being educated in—and whether this was a conscious or inertial decision. And as we all know, the question of what we are being taught in the Arab world has been an issue of international and regional concern from 9/11 onward, as well as since the publication of the UN Human Development Reports.

The reality is that these historical presentations are choices that have been made. They are choices made by writers of our schoolbooks, and choices of our ministries of education, and choices of our governments. They are also the choices of our religious authorities who have decided to focus on the more militant aspects of Arab and Islamic history. As though all life in the seventh, eighth, and ninth centuries was filled with warriors and military campaigns. We are deprived of the mass of information that could have been included in our history, ranging from social and economic questions, to geographic and philosophical aspects of historical investigation. Often, we are presented with very fixed ideas of what it means to be a good Muslim.

THE CHALLENGE OF FREEDOM

Dear Saif,

When many of our fellow Muslims talk about the West, we hear them saying that the West has no values, that anything goes. We hear that everyone is free to do whatever they want. Often this is taken to mean that men and women are free to have sex with each other without commitments, and outside of marriage, or that children have no respect for their parents. It goes almost without saying that the West is seen as Godless.

Let me say immediately that I do not agree with this view. Our lives, yours and mine, are deeply intertwined with that of the West. In fact, I believe firmly that we are constructed out of elements from the East and the West. It is impossible to reject one for the other, because it would mean rejecting part of ourselves, part of our own perception.

But before I get too involved in the question of how

we are deeply related to the West, I want to hone in on this idea that the West has no values, and that freedom is a license for sin and decadence.

This is the basic idea that we often have as Muslims: freedom is license, and license means anything goes. It means that you can and will take drugs and have random anonymous sexual relations with everyone. As though it were so simple. I am generalizing, of course, but there is a certain strain of Islamic thought or prejudice that believes this.

In recent history, one of the key thinkers behind modern extremist Islam, Sayed Qutb, propagated these ideas. Qutb was a prolific Egyptian writer who was imprisoned in Egypt in the 1950s and 1960s, and executed in 1966. He started out as a literary critic with a passion for Arabic poetry. Quite a romantic soul. He was very well known and highly regarded. He was sent to the United States to further his studies, and spent a total of two years there. He seems not to have enjoyed his time there. Who knows why. He spent his time in a small college in the Midwest. He returned to Egypt with a changed attitude. From his writings of this time you can view him either as extremely pious and devout or as bitter and frustrated. He recounts with horror and disgust how he witnessed dances that involved men and women, and his descriptions of bare flesh carry an almost erotic tone. Was Qutb mesmerized or was he disgusted? Was he devoutly moral or was he confused by his own urges? He was certainly unable to understand how this world of the Midwest was in any way related to the little village he came from in Egypt.

Qutb was an extremely fluent and persuasive writer. I have spent time reading his main work, which is an immense collection called *In the Shade of the Quran,* which can be read as a set of thoughts or musings on the Quran. It is an extremely important work. There is a general rule in the Islamic tradition that only suitably qualified scholars are allowed to compose interpretations and explanations of the Quran. This sounds logical. He who is qualified writes about what he knows.

Then there is another category of writings that has found favor with a new generation of readers. These are the "musings" that have been composed by people who want to share the thoughts they have had while being inspired by reading verses of the Quran. It seems clear from reading the various "musings" that such a format provides more leeway in how the ideas of the Quran can be expressed.

What is fascinating about Sayed Qutb's musings is that he writes fluently and at times mesmerizingly, and at the same time strays from the text he is discussing quite radically. At times there seems to be no connection between the text of the Quran he allegedly is discussing and what he is saying.

His writing is entrancing, and unmoored. Dangerous—in a word. I read him reluctantly and with great trepidation.

I trace my own initial interaction with the theme that freedom is license to Qutb and others who followed him. In some circles, his word is taken for granted. Qutb becomes the explainer to those within the Muslim faith about how Western society operates. His views are repeated without even referring to him anymore. It is as though the ideas have seeped into our collective understanding without verification. The view equates freedom with license and moral decadence.

I have wondered about this. I too spent many years in the West, including New York and London. Is it fair to equate freedom with license? Or freedom with decadence? I admit that initially I was confused. I did not understand the approach that said you as an individual are free to choose what you do in your life, and what you do with your life. It made me feel exposed and vulnerable. For the first time I felt that I had no boundaries. I felt that I could not tell what was permitted from what was not allowed. Instinctively I would wonder if something was allowed or not. I would always lean toward not doing something if I had any doubts. Perhaps this was my cautious nature. I look back and think it was more likely the result of having been told repeatedly over the years that things were haram, or prohibited, by the principles and rules of Islam.

I wondered how other people organized their time, how they made choices, how they knew what they liked or did not like. I was fascinated by the idea of being able to do what you want, rather than being told to do what you have to do.

I did not find it easy at all. As I say, it caused me a lot of stress and tension. I kept to myself mostly, moving repeatedly toward and away from devotion and prayer. Sometimes I would cling to the Quran, and listen to the recordings of recitations that I had brought with me. Sometimes I threw caution to the wind and did things because I could.

After three years at school in the United Kingdom, under a fairly strict regimen, I made it to university. I was eighteen years old. I did not quite know it then, but I was about to be faced with freedom. I did not even have to attend classes. I was free to stay up all night and sleep all day if I wanted. I could drink and smoke and spend time with girls. I was completely free to do as I pleased with my time. I asked my new friends why this was the case. I spoke about it to my teachers. I was told that as a young adult I was considered mature enough to organize my own time, and my own course of research. Like all my fellow students of law, I would have a one-hour meeting with my professor a week, in which we would discuss the research I had done beforehand. Lectures were given every day, but we were free to attend or not.

I did not last long in this new state. I had no idea how to organize myself and my time. I had no idea where and how I could build structure. I was not even sure structure was what was missing. I simply did not know. On top of this, I was frustrated by my inability to successfully seduce the women I wanted to seduce. And this pushed me further into a cocoon of solitary smoking and listening to the Quran. By the Easter holidays, I'd had enough. I was now in the grip of a full depression. I knew that I did not know what to do with myself.

I decided to go to Mecca. It was the holy month of Ramadan, when we fast from sunrise till sunset. The period of ten days that I spent in Mecca was the most intense period of devotion and prayer that I have ever experienced. The holy mosque is lit up with huge spotlights all night long, and there are hundreds of thousands of pilgrims all dressed in white twenty-four hours a day. There is no difference between you and anyone else. In the basin of the mosque, you feel that you are close to Allah. You are at the beating heart of Islam. I prayed and prayed and prayed. In between I read the Quran. I watched others praying. All kinds of

human beings make it to Mecca. You feel the
universality and the power of Islam.

I decided in my heart that I wanted to stay in Mecca.
I decided not to go back to university. Here was the
right place for me. What better than to devote my life
to the study of the Quran and the sayings of the
Prophet? I would grow a long beard and wear a black
cloak. I would one day be recognized as a scholar and
people would sit around me and listen attentively as I
explained various points of Islamic faith and law.

And then I woke up. I knew that this was me
running away from all the questions that were troubling
me back at university. I realized that living in Mecca
was an escapist fantasy. In fact, it became clear to me
then that the real challenge as a Muslim was not to run
away from the West and seek comfort at the heart of
Islam. The real challenge was to figure out the structure
that would allow me to exist out there as a Muslim.

As the years went by, I continued to think about
freedom and structure. I came to understand that the
perception that freedom is decadence is a fictitious one.
Freedom is a good that is preserved and defended
because it places individual responsibility at the heart of
society. Freedom is not presented as a gift to self-
destruct or to engage in immoral acts out of principle.
Freedom is a gift to use your will and perception to
impose a moral structure on yourself. Without the

freedom to choose our path, we are morally crippled. It becomes someone else—on earth—who directs our moral choices. Is this being fully accepting of your faith? Or are we only fully accepting of our faith when we are free to reject it, as is possible in Western liberal democracies? I now see the subtlety of freedom. Freedom is not a license for decadence. Freedom is the highest partner in the construction of a moral world.

OUR COMPLEX ENTANGLEMENT
WITH THE WEST

Saif,

I want you to consider the tremendous invasion of ideas, experiences, histories, and worldviews that entered our Arab and Muslim world over the last two centuries, starting with Napoleon's invasion of Egypt in 1798. Up until then the Arab world had been a quiet backwater that had no experience of Western technological supremacy.

You will have to research this matter yourself. I want you to think about what the appearance and demonstration of new objects and ideas does to a people who have been secluded in their own world for centuries.

It acts as a shock to the worldview that any people has of itself. This applies to the Arabs and Muslims in 1798, just as it applied to the Aztecs when the Spaniards came to Mexico, or to the Native Americans when the first settlers from Europe arrived on the North American continent.

Worldviews that survived untouched and unchanged, and in a sense pure, were turned upside down by questions that no one had thought of before, such as perhaps that sexuality is not chosen but discovered, or that people are thinking rational intelligent beings rather than sheep to be guided by clerics. There are questions that we do not ask, such as what it means to see the world through the eyes of women rather than men, or that perhaps it is better to educate women rather than leave them only to the realm of the home. There are questions that we need to ask about what we really mean by justice—whether economic or social. There are questions about what it means to be weak in a world of technological and industrial giants such as the United States and China. We have questions such as the possibility of a different approach to relations between males and females. We have questions about whether a supposedly moral society is better than a healthy society, whether politics and ethics can or should be separated, whether there is knowledge that is separate from religious knowledge, how we might behave if we did not have oil wealth.

But just because a society and a culture have not produced a particular set of questions does not mean that they do not have the ability to recognize new and foreign questions as relevant.

Our Islamic world has been struggling with the idea of what is true and authentically Muslim alongside what must be rejected as foreign.

Why do we do this? Why do we insist that there are puzzles and questions that do not apply to us? Of course we instinctively want to maintain that we are different, that we are better, that we have answered these questions in our own way and therefore there is no need for foreign ideas to help us.

But is this really the case? Have we really answered these questions? I keep mentioning questions and answers, but I have not named them.

What is remarkable is that these are all questions that we know surface in our Islamic societies and yet we push them away with the claim that we are different and that these are foreign questions. The most important justification for the claim that these questions are foreign is that other societies have taken many steps to begin to answer these questions.

These are brave and courageous steps, even if we do not like the answers provided. Rather than condemning Western society in particular for having examined and theorized these matters, we should open our eyes and ears to the fact that we share these problems.

What we face within our Islamic communities today

is mostly a reaction to the fact that the questions are out in the open, and we can no longer hide from them. This explains to me why we have a rising push toward the simplifying and simplistic Salafi worldview, which is the view that looks to those early Muslims (Salafis) of the Prophet's era and the two generations of Muslims who followed. It is a desire to return to the certainties of seventh- and eighth-century Islam. The purity signified by this early era of Islam is held up to be a possibility for Muslims in the twenty-first century. It is an imagined group that we are all invited to return to, by some of the most ferocious Islamist groups of the day, such as ISIS, Jabhat al-Nusra, and Al Qaeda. The invitation is to remove ourselves from the twenty-first century, and the reality that we and the foreign are no longer separable, and to return to a mythical state of pious nonknowledge.

What do I mean by pious nonknowledge? I mean the state where we pretend that by ignoring the questions, and the issues that led to these questions, we can somehow remove this knowledge from our minds. This includes questions around sexuality, gender equality, political and social rights, and the right to discover yourself rather than comply with the ideals of the community. We know that other societies and other religions have faced these questions and have developed many different answers. Perhaps some of these answers are relevant to our lives as Muslims as well? And remember that knowledge does not consist simply of answers. Great knowledge consists of being familiar with the questions, the doubts, the possibility that things might be different.

The truth that you must become accustomed to is that this world of ideas that have no specific religion or ethnicity or even loyalty is not a world to accept or reject. It is like eating. Whatever you consume must be digested. There is no other way. These ideas, once comprehended, must be absorbed and perhaps modified, intellectually or emotionally, to suit your identity and perspective. The reality of non-Muslim ideas and concepts and technologies being a part of one's existence—physically, philosophically, politically—is something that will prove to be a great challenge and yet fruitful in the long run.

In the twenty-first century, it is still unusual for Arabs and Muslims to think of the very dynamic and mixed relationship we share with the West. In almost all ways, we in the Muslim world are organically linked to the West, and we might make better sense of ourselves if we realize these connections. A result of these connections economically, through the sale of hydrocarbons or through our import of immense quantities of consumer and industrial products, is that our lives are increasingly not just livable but pleasurable as well. This opens up an interesting confrontation that is probably best, and sadly, exemplified in the way

Islamic fundamentalists reject every ounce of Western civilization and yet freeload on Western consumer items and Western technological innovations.

It is this deep inconsistency that needs to be resolved between our anti-Western narratives as propagated by Arab nationalist and Islamist movements, and the reality of our deep reliance on one another. It is interesting to note that we are intertwined with the West in ways in which the West is not intertwined with us. It is perplexing to hear a fundamentalist criticizing the West but then observe him counting his money in dollars. Is it not deeply incoherent to damn the West but to trust only the U.S. dollar as a currency in our Orwellian "disputed area" of the Middle East?

Saif, I believe it is important for us, you and me, to recognize at the level of our daily language and conversation that we need to be consistent between the products we use and the systems that produced them— between the physical world around us and the ideas that underlie them.

But more about language later.

REVELATION AND REASON

Habeebie Saif,

We often insist on our particularity. We love the idea of
being unique. We imagine that we are the only people
who have ever tasted suffering. We fantasize that only
we understand spirituality or that only we have a
historic purpose. We denigrate others and elevate
our own pain above all else. And so when we have
questions, we insist that these questions are specific and
unique to our situation. We believe that no one else can
begin to comprehend our situation, let alone offer a
solution.

You will find, as I have, that we Muslims are no
different from those of other faiths in this inward-looking
approach. We know that Allah revealed his final message
for humanity to our Prophet Mohammed, and we pride
ourselves on this fact.

There is a debate that took place about a thousand

years ago that has had the effect of locking us Muslims into the position of particularity rather than universality.

As in the period immediately after the Prophet's passing, the early Muslims engaged in collecting the various verses of the Quran into a single manuscript and began producing copies. They also spent time and energy collecting the sayings of the Prophet. With the expansion of Islam through proselytization and wars of conquest, the early Muslims came into contact with non-Muslims of various faiths. They also came across different traditions of knowledge. In particular, they came across Christians who were well versed in the works of the Greek philosophers, Plato and Aristotle in particular.

In engaging with these new subjects, and in many cases, with these new entrants to Islam, the early Arab Muslims came across many new ideas.

Islam developed by posing questions that arose from within the Islamic faith, but crucially, it also developed by responding to the questions posed by non-Muslims and the greats of Greek philosophy. How did this come about? The early Muslims realized that non-Muslim subjects were able to challenge the call of Islam with very sophisticated arguments. So in order to persuade these non-Muslims to accept Islam, the early Muslims had to become acquainted with the logic and debating methods of other cultures.

What were some of the questions? Do they have any relevance to our lives as Muslims today? Well, a basic question arose due to the recognition of the early Muslims that the Quran and the sayings of the Prophet did not cover every question that might arise on moral and ethical conduct. How were the early Muslims to resolve this problem? How were they to fill the gaps? One set of Islamic thinkers said that they would stick with the texts they possessed. Another set of Islamic thinkers said that if Allah and the Prophet had left spaces, then these spaces should be filled by the application of human logic and reason. This became the great conflict between those representing Reason—meaning human logic—and those representing Revelation. Remember, revelation refers to what has been revealed by Allah. This debate took place in a tense and heated political environment.

Why did this debate arise in the first place? What were some of the gaps? Well, let us take a look at the world of power and politics. The Quran does not lay out a political system for Muslims to follow. Does this mean that there is no need for a political system? The Prophet was a religious leader as well as a military and political leader. How would the early Muslims work out what happened when faced with political questions? How was the leader of the Muslim community to be chosen? How was power to be transferred from one leader to the next?

How were errors to be corrected? How was opposition or disagreement to be expressed?

In today's environment, the questions might be more like: How do we make sure that political power is not misused? Does political power need to be given to one individual, or is power something that can exist in many places?

For one reason or another, those representing only Revelation won the debate. Those representing Reason were persecuted and hounded until their school of thought became a faint trace in the thousand years of history since then.

It is fascinating to observe the consequences of a debate that took place a thousand years ago. These consequences are roiling the Arab world and the broader Islamic world today. The role of reason has been eclipsed. It is forever associated with the Greek philosophers as well as the so-called Mutazilites—the Muslim thinkers who supported a primary role for logic and reason in understanding the Divine Will.

Unfortunately in today's Arab world, and in the Arabic language, the word *falsafah,* which means "philosophy," is a dirty word. It is seen as a distraction from the importance of keeping the faith pure and unsullied by questions that will only serve to divide and separate the Muslims.

My view is that the questions asked by the early

philosophers, both Muslim and non-Muslim, are questions that emerge in all societies in one way or another. The treasures that the Arab Muslims once translated into Arabic and possessed as intellectual capital were a means to continually refine our understanding of those fundamental questions. By turning our backs on the philosophers, we attempted to close our minds to the questions. We attempted to lock ourselves into our special and separate world of Quranic Revelation.

But questions have the odd habit of reappearing. And they have certainly reappeared in the modern technological, globalized world you and I live in.

The question of Reason and Revelation is one that we need to pose openly and bravely. We also need to consider the answers that other faiths have developed over the last thousand years. Remember that for a thousand years we have tried hard to ignore these questions. Other faiths also faced turmoil in confronting these questions. How did they answer them? If the questions are the same in each faith, then we as Muslims will benefit from an exploration of the answers those faiths produced and continue to produce.

Will this threaten the integrity and cohesion of the Islamic community, as many of our clerics feared and continue to fear? I think that the process of addressing these issues will open up the possibility of greater integrity and cohesion. We deepen our faith, as well as our understanding of our faith, by asking such questions. What you must do while asking these questions is to maintain your faith that there are good and vital answers out there.

What do we as Muslims lose as we consider other people's answers to the same questions? Do we lose our faith? Does our faith become tainted? Do we become less Muslim because we found better explanations elsewhere? Hardly. On the contrary, we discover a depth to our own faith when we open our eyes to the universality of our condition. We discover that Islam has within it the capacity and resources to accommodate all types of ideas and intellectual challenges. We take greater pride in the universal nature of our faith.

What has changed in all these years is that I became clearer about the questions that we share as human beings irrespective of religion. This is already some consolation. When I was your age, I was still coming to terms with the idea that there could be questions about such important matters. At that time, it was taboo even to suggest that you had questions, let alone voice them. In today's world, the questions come charging at us every day from all directions. The questions that you will have will likely have to do with those who are not of your faith. How should we maintain our identity as Muslims, and deal with others who are not of our faith?

This question of identity is a question faced by many other faiths. It is the question of exclusivity and its implications.

There are other questions relating to how we should deal with violence, and what place ancient violence has in our modern understanding of Islam. Again, other faiths such as Christianity and Judaism have dealt extensively with the experience of violence, as perpetrators and as victims, as well as the theory of violence in religion and society. Let us look at their literature and see what our clerics might be missing or may have overlooked. There are many different ways to perceive the world today. We are no longer desert tribes, or villagers on the periphery of great events. We are all deeply enmeshed in the modern world with its different stories, experiences, and demands. How can we stretch ancient concepts and attitudes without destroying our emotional and mental understandings? Should we turn back to our past, closing our eyes to what we can learn from others, insisting that we are special and different from all others?

I suppose I started this letter with these thoughts because it has taken me years to uncover the truth that the questions at the heart of our faith are also questions that have been asked in other faiths, and by other people. I want you to open your mind to the full range of positions and arguments within Islam. By this I mean the arguments and positions of the different, often warring, sects of Islam today, as well as the schools of thought that have faded away over the centuries. Remember when I took you and your younger brother to see the professor of Islamic law in Los Angeles when you were thirteen? His house had been converted into a home for lost books. There was hardly any space for him or his family to live. He showed us the thousands and thousands of books that he had collected over a lifetime of study. He told us about the ancient texts that he had acquired that outlined approaches taken by early Muslims that have faded from memory. These are arguments that had been put forth by our predecessors. And were they any less Muslim for having explored ideas? For having asked questions? For having considered possibilities?

I want you to look at the theological literature of Judaism and Christianity, as well as that of Buddhism and Hinduism. I want you to read the great works of philosophy left to us by the Greeks but also by the Arabs. I want you to open your eyes and mind to the philosophers of the world throughout the centuries. There is tremendous value in acquainting yourself with the questions this literature attempts to resolve. In fact, you will find the subtlety of human perception overwhelming. And when a friendly Muslim cleric tells you that reading such literature is wrong, tell him that you can only know it is wrong after having read and understood it. There is no knowledge that is wrong. Only knowledge that is difficult, troubling, enlightening, liberating, and intoxicating.

Your friendly cleric will tell you that everything is already in Islam. And he will be telling you the truth. But you can tell him that human perception is not equally distributed and that you want to discover how others have perceived the world around us. Perhaps their descriptions will help you align yourself with your faith even more than before. I find this to be the real gift of others—the elegance of their perceptions, the labor that has been put into developing interesting positions, and the perfection of expression. Just as you read fiction in order to discover the names for emotions and experiences that we have all had, you read the philosophy and theology of others in order to enrich your own perceptions.

And finally, if your friendly cleric tells you that everything has been answered in the texts of our forefathers, you can tell him that you believe that every generation of Muslims should reexamine their faith and their understanding in the terms that they understand. You and your generation were formed, and constituted, at the start of the twenty-first century. Your minds are a mix of ideas, habits, traditions, and the effects of technologies and travel that would have made no sense to Muslims in the 1950s, let alone in the tenth century or the seventh century. You and your friends need to reexpress Islam in the words and the needs of your generation. Different lived realities compel us to change focus and to rearrange priorities.

So I end this letter with a choice for you. You can choose to live as a Muslim who insists that only Muslims are able to have knowledge, wisdom, and understanding. Or you can choose to find knowledge, wisdom, and understanding in all cultures, literatures, and philosophies. You can choose to be locked into a particular world, or you can set forth into a world of human experience.

SERMONS AND WHAT TO EXPECT
IN THE MOSQUE ON FRIDAYS

Habeebie Saif,

When I was your age, I would go to the mosque on Fridays. The communal prayer was always an opportunity to feel connected with other people of all types. We would line up in rows, rich and poor alike, and we would go through the prostrations and recitals required of Muslims. Before the prayer started, we would all sit facing the front of the mosque and listen to the imam, or prayer leader, deliver his weekly sermon. Most of the time, I did not understand what he was saying. My Arabic language knowledge was not very strong. The parts I did understand usually involved the invocations to Allah to protect Muslims around the globe and defeat the enemies of Islam. My memory of these visits to Friday prayers is a mixed one. The beauty of prayer and communal worship, as we all prostrated in unison, whispering the prayers and verses of the Quran that form part of the event—I cherish this memory. But the violence and aggression of the sermon was something that my friends and I would always wonder about. This has become a very serious topic around the Muslim world since, and you can visit mosques today where the tone has changed significantly.

I was fifteen when I first went to boarding school in the UK. I headed to the mosque on the first Friday— our day of rest and the day for communal prayers— instead of going to chapel, as the other children did. This was the understanding that I had with the school.

My fellow Muslim schoolmates and I made our way down the suburban roads of the school's town. The houses got smaller and smaller as we progressed. The neighborhood was clearly not well-to-do. Finally, one of my friends pointed out the house that had been designated as a mosque. Small, residential, and made of red brick. It was one of a hundred cookie-cutter houses of suburban England. We took our shoes off before stepping into the brightly lit interior. The house had been converted by having key walls removed to make way for a large prayer room. Multicolored silky Chinese-manufactured prayer mats were lined up untidily. We muttered shy greetings to the already gathered attendees. They were all dressed in South Asian clothes and seemed to know one another well. All older than us.

I came away from that suburban mosque shocked at what seemed to be an extremely violent Islam. While the sermon was being conducted in a language I did not understand, but believe to have been Bengali, I was given little leaflets with machine guns drawn on them and injunctions to kill various Arab leaders.

Once the prayer was over, I returned to my school and asked to see the head teacher in charge of the boarding house where I was assigned to live.

I was somewhat embarrassed and did not know where to start. I told him about my experience at the local mosque and confessed that I did not feel comfortable at all going back there. I did not go into too much detail. He did not ask too many questions. He suggested I could attend chapel instead. I was a bit taken aback. Why did he think I should go to a Christian service? Why couldn't I just sit in an empty classroom and wait for everyone else to join me after chapel?

For some reason he persuaded me that it was not a religious experience for all who attended. It was one way of connecting with the community of the school and the other students in a context outside of the classroom. He also pointed out that during chapel the school sometimes made important announcements for the student body.

I listened carefully and later came back to him agreeing that I would attend the chapel service. Why would I make this decision? I can imagine the horror of people back at home if they knew of this. In fact, even today, as a certain class of Muslim finds out that I, a Muslim, attended a Christian service, they will be shocked and question the integrity of my faith.

But look at why I did it, and why I have no regrets. I certainly did not attend chapel out of any religious belief but simply out of fear of my own community. Sad to say, but what I saw and heard in the local mosque near my school did not seem to be the appropriate way to worship and build community. And I certainly did not see the mosque as the correct place for such propaganda. Why should I go to a mosque where I am encouraged to immerse myself in an ill-thought-out war against all?

My feelings about that mosque were very strong and continue till today. I felt those at the mosque made a mockery of our religion. They took a public space for Muslims of all nationalities and they converted it into a squalid den for a particularly ignorant and violent program. They narrowed the space, in which I had expected to pray and find solace, into a camp for barefoot and uneducated would-be warriors. My fellow Muslims in the area had either chosen or allowed for this conversion of a public space from a space of generosity and calm to one of anger and violence.

I made the decision that day that what I found

available and was on offer as the Muslim place of communal prayer was not acceptable to me as a Muslim. As I look back on that day, almost thirty years ago, I realize now what I did not realize fully then. I realize that I had made an almost conscious decision that the way we express our Islam is the result of a set of choices. And that these choices are based on how we view the world.

Certainly, the mosque that day represented a Muslim perspective. But did it need to be so narrow, vicious, and angry? Did it need to be violent, aggressive, and ignorant? I do not think so. Did it represent all of Islam in all of its beauty? Certainly not. It represented an Islam that was impoverished by its practitioners. Do you understand these words? I am rereading them myself: "an Islam that was impoverished by its practitioners." This means that I believe that we have a duty, that we are called upon, to bring our highest and best qualities to Islam as we practice it. If we do not, the deficiency is not within Islam, the deficiency is within us as people who have not thought deeply enough, or tried hard enough, to make sense of the disparate factors pulling on us.

I attended chapel with the rest of the school from then on. Did I pray? No, I didn't. Did I see decadence and an absence of morality in chapel? Not at all. I did listen to the sermons. And I found that they differed from the fiery sermons I had heard in mosques since I was a child. Here again, I believe that we should experience the perspectives of other faiths in order to reflect on our own. It is through observing the sermons in a church that I began to imagine that perhaps our mosque sermons might be presented in a different way.

One clear idea I came away with was that faith and community go together. It is part of the package, Saif. That is why sermons are common in religious communities. The faithful are addressed. Different faiths have different ideas about how the community should be guided, advised, encouraged, and directed. I cannot help thinking that the sermons I heard, and you heard, in the Arab world are more a product of inertia and habit than of a conscious decision. It is the weight of words that have been passed down from one generation to the next without thought as to what we could say differently.

What might you find today in the mosques back at home? Well, the government had to get involved and begin to set standards and expectations regarding what preachers could say in the mosques on Fridays. Preachers are no longer allowed to encourage violence. They are not allowed to encourage hate. They are no longer allowed to condemn those of other faiths. We as a community came together and decided that we as

Muslims had a right to demand of our religious leaders that they put their energy into more productive sermons. In place of the anger and violence that was clearly the result of poor training and inertia across the decades, we now have preachers who talk about constructive values. They speak about what people can do to assist one another. They explain the more difficult passages of the Quran, or they demonstrate the hidden wisdom in one of the sayings of the Prophet. Nowadays, when the Friday prayer and sermon are over, you leave the mosque with a sense of quiet pride instead of anger and irritation. Nowadays you can safely head to the mosque, knowing that you will be uplifted rather than manipulated, as seemed to happen in the past.

Not all governments in Muslim-majority countries have succeeded in directing religious discourse. It is a difficult area to regulate and monitor. Not all preaching takes place in mosques, and there are unofficial sites where people can gather and listen to radical preachers. Finally, there are many speeches and sermons by radicals who have been detained or even killed that are available online. If you want to hear the sermons of radical Islam, it is difficult for any government to stop you.

As we progress, we will further develop our communal ideas of the purposes and possibilities of the Friday sermon.

GOOD DEEDS AND BAD DEEDS

Habeebie Saif,

I remember when I was your age the importance of the idea of *hassanat* and *sayiat*. Good deeds and bad deeds is how I would put this in English. These were and remain very powerful words that resonate in my mind every day. I still mentally count things as good deeds and bad deeds. Many of the questions that we used to ask as children revolved around how many *hassanat* something was worth. When we considered our actions, we would think of the two angels perched one on each shoulder, scribbling down our good deeds and our bad deeds. On the Day of Judgment, these angels would be called forward to present the deeds of our life. Allah's judgment would involve weighing the good deeds against the bad.

This would make sense to a child in any society.

The point-scoring approach is one familiar in many religions, and in many of life's pursuits. You will even find very wealthy businesspeople saying that earning large amounts of money is about keeping track of their success. It's a way of making sure you are doing well. So point-scoring has its purposes and its functions. I believe it has its place within our faith because it allows us to give relative weights to different actions. It allows us to prioritize certain actions over others. It certainly points us in the direction of ethical behavior.

Sometimes, though, I think that we need to rethink how to look at the points system. Remember that though Allah's system is perfect, we human beings are not. Our psychology develops or regresses depending on how you look at human development. If at the time of the Prophet, the points system was perfectly fitted to the early Muslims, in the twenty-first century we may need to rethink how we incorporate it into our lives.

I am going to give you an example to think about. If you look through the sayings of the Prophet, you will find a number of chapter headings under which the sayings are collected. These chapter headings reflect the concerns of people in the rocky deserts of Mecca and Medina in the seventh century. The types of issues covered can be listed straightforwardly. They include rules on ablution (ritual cleansing before prayer), fasting, prayer, zakat (charitable giving), and business dealings.

These categories cover a few thousand sayings of the

Prophet—as recognized by Sunni Islam. Shia Islam recognizes and uses far fewer sayings, since the way the Shia verify the veracity of the sayings differs from the Sunni method.

The sayings also include references, on occasion, to the idea of how many *hassanat* a person can accumulate for undertaking certain acts, or uttering certain verses of the Quran, or other invocations.

In our age, you are going to come across people who only look at the world in terms of *hassanat* and *sayiat*. They paint every action, and thought, in terms of black or white, permitted or not permitted. And they count—most probably subconsciously—the good points that they are collecting throughout the day.

Where does this take us? How far does it move us in the direction of morally worthy acts? I find that it is useful in so far as it points us in the right direction. However, it also limits us if we don't think about it more broadly. If you expand the use of *hassanat* and *sayiat* to all spheres of life, you tend to forget about appreciating the moment in which you are living, and you enter a kind of moral accounting or arithmetic of religion.

Now you might think that this is noble and worthy—and it is. But don't forget that accounting for things in life is a way of keeping track of activity. The importance of life is not the accounting but the activities that we engage in. Don't be a moral penny-pincher. If you are focused on the general arc of your moral life, no amount of *hassanat* will be able to compete with a life lived with uncounted acts of kindness and generosity. Rather than counting your *hassanat*, give of your goodness freely. The points system is a framework and a starting point, but imagine how generous a person can be if he or she is not counting the points they gain by doing certain acts. If you can let go of your personal ethical point-scoring, then you will likely have reached a higher ethical state within Islam.

Think of the system of *hassanat* and *sayiat* as the framework for your principled and selfless action. Points fit in well with the question-and-answer approach to moral conduct, which uses questions such as, Is this halal or haram—allowed by Islam or not? The balanced, principled person I want you to become no longer needs to ask these questions because he or she has absorbed the appropriate principles of behavior. In this state, you know the elegant and consistent way in which Allah's principles operate in new and diverse spheres of life that no one in seventh-century Arabia could have imagined. At this stage of knowledge and behavior, I expect you to be and feel more complete. And your values are more integrated with one another and displayed in your daily actions, rather than in just your daily accounting.

THE QURAN AND THE SEARCH
FOR KNOWLEDGE

Habeebie Saif,
You know how much I love our library at home. It is
where I feel most at peace with myself and the world.
Our whole family likes this room.

Whenever friends or guests come over to our house, I
like to show them the library. I am not entirely sure
why. In some ways it is a very private place. It is like a
window to my mind. If you look at the books on the
shelves, and piled up on the table, you can get an idea of
what I like to think about. You are able to access my
deepest interests. It is an exposed position to be in. You
know I have all kinds of books there, from the Talmud
in Hebrew and Arabic to the Quran in many languages;
from books on Western philosophy to the advanced
mathematics textbooks I bought in the hopes of gaining
a deeper understanding of all of those wonderful
squiggles that add up to mathematical knowledge.

Libraries have been key institutions in many societies around the world. The Library of Alexandria was one of the most famous libraries in history. The Muslim world still feels the pain of the destruction of our libraries when the Mongols sacked Baghdad in the thirteenth century. We read the horrifying accounts of how our accumulated knowledge was tipped into the Tigris River. The water turned black from the ink of all the manuscripts and books that were destroyed during that dark time.

Public libraries have been seen as a good that communities and societies benefit from. There are programs establishing public libraries in many countries. Whenever I visit New York, I look with envy and pride at the magnificent building housing the New York Public Library. On entering this beautiful structure, you will be struck by the grandeur of the place. You will wonder how a people could have spent and invested so much in order to house books.

You will remember the many times when I spoke about the need for libraries in the Arab world where we live. They are coming. More and more people are talking about the idea.

Private libraries are a luxury. My library is a true luxury and privilege. I know that the world's information is now available online. This was an argument people used and continue to use against physical libraries with physical books. But there is a slight problem with this argument. Though many books are available in digital format, and more is being done to digitize books, there are still many books that are not digitized, or if they are, are not available without paying large sums in order to have access to them. The e-books that have taken the world of publishing by storm have certainly opened up the world of knowledge and literature to a greater readership, but this does not mean that the physical book will be replaced entirely.

There is also an important aspect to the physical presence of a book, which you can feel and smell and write notes all over. The physical book can, if you spend enough time with it, become a physical–intellectual extension of yourself.

I like few things better than to mark my books with ink. I love to scribble in the margins. I review these notes over the years, and from the style in which I wrote, I can tell if I was excited or tired, angry or calm. These are important signals for the memory. It places the page in a context of emotion and ideas.

Visitors to our home library always ask me if I have read all the books we have. I used to feel uncomfortable with this question. I felt that I should be able to answer positively, that yes, I have read every single book in that room. But this will never be the case. There are simply too many. What I love is to know that if I have a question in the middle of the night, I can go down to our library and I am likely to find a sequence of books that will cover the history of the matter from different angles and give a philosophical review of the key issues. Why would this be the case? Well, because I do not just buy books; I collect them with the idea that they fit into a pattern of knowledge. The more specialized the knowledge, the more difficult the subject matter. But my level of interest is more general. I am interested in the way other cultures answer general questions of life.

I used to wonder why an Arab or a Muslim would ever read a work on ancient Roman history. I used to be astonished when a fellow student at university would tell me that they were going to spend three or four years of their lives dedicated to the history of the ancient world. Why would anyone waste their time? Anyhow, what did this have to do with my life as a Muslim? Surely I had better things to do with my time. I was interested in moral questions, and these would be answered by reference to the Quran.

And if I were going to read history, then I should read histories related to the Arab or Muslim worlds.

In your travels, physically or online, you will come across many fellow Muslims who will tell you that this is the appropriate approach. We, the Muslims, are known as People of the Book. The Jews and the Christians are also in the same category. But I am never sure what this means practically for them, from our point of view. Do we accept the Old and New Testaments? Are we to read them? Are we to learn from them? The answer to this question varies. Often we are told that the Old and New Testaments were changed and therefore have no legitimacy anymore. This is why we have the Quran. Others will say that you are permitted to read these texts but only if you are a scholar.

In any case, the direction I want to take you in is the one where you are told that the only book you need to read in this life is the Quran.

Let me be clear. The Quran is a special book. It is our special book. It is cherished by us and our fellow Muslims as the word of Allah as revealed to his Messenger the Prophet Mohammed. We know the story of how the first words of the Quran were revealed to the Prophet by the Angel Gabriel in the dark cave where the Prophet would go to meditate.

The Quran was revealed in the same way over the next two decades. The Prophet transmitted the Quran as a recited text to the early Muslims. They in turn memorized it. And as I have told you in other letters, the Quran has been transmitted in unchanged written form since that time. This is to be wondered at, and admired. We all take pride in the preservation of the unchanging word of Allah.

There is a wealth of knowledge and a treasury of wisdom contained in the verses of the Quran. Read the Quran and think through the words. If you are honest with yourself, you will find that there is much that you will not understand, and there will be much that puzzles you. You will not be the first Muslim to have this reaction.

In fact, the first Muslims also had difficulties. They were closer in time to the Prophet and the Revelation, and so they were bolder than we are today. They embarked on collecting words and their meanings from the people around them. These were the first dictionaries of the Arabic language. They knew that words had multiple meanings, and they needed to map them out. Then they began to look at the Quran from the perspective of multiple meanings. They started to write commentaries on the Quran explaining to less educated people what particular words meant or referred to. They began to interpret the Quran. They began to reveal aspects of the Quran that were not initially clear, or that had meanings that were less literal than initially thought.

This period was an intellectually rich period. It was one of finding meaning in many ways. People began to ask questions about what was not covered in the Quran. The Quran is a slim book by modern standards. It can cover many aspects of life, but it necessarily leaves much untouched.

So the early scholars of Islam began to collect memories. These were memories of the followers of the Prophet from his earliest days. They collected what are now known as the sayings of the Prophet. These are collections of memories, numbering in the thousands, covering many aspects of life. You will find topics such as the way in which to pray, and how to prepare for prayer. Others cover matters such as kindness, and generosity. Others will baffle you unless you again have access to an explanation and interpretation.

So you see? The Quran is the holy book of Islam, but it requires other books to explain it. Those books in turn need books to place them in a context.

This is the primary argument to make to those who say that one should read only the Quran, for it has all knowledge within it. It has the key message of Allah. But even the Prophet is widely known for having encouraged us to go, even to China, in the search for knowledge.

This Chinese saying of the Prophet is one of those very powerful sayings because it establishes a point that should structure our lives as Muslims. The Chinese saying does not tell us what kind of knowledge to seek. It does not determine in advance what we should be looking for. It talks of knowledge.

It is also important because it tells us to travel, not to make war, but to seek and acquire knowledge from other cultures—cultures that have nothing to do with our way of life. It is an invitation to mix with others and open our minds to them. This is in stark contrast to what many people will insist on in today's Muslim world. Many insist that we stick only to what we know has an early Islamic source. We are told to focus on the pedigree of our ideas, and not on the quality of an idea, which could come to us from anywhere.

In the search for knowledge, if we are honest with ourselves, we will find that knowledge is the common property of all of humanity. Those who truly seek knowledge will find it, not only in the religious literature of Islam, but also in the textbooks of Western history, in the writing of philosophers of all stripes, in the holy texts of other religions. We will and must seek knowledge that will allow us to reflect more deeply on ourselves as Muslims and as human beings. This is the kind of approach I believe is deeply Islamic, and the one I ask you to undertake.

This search for knowledge is fundamental to the nature of our religion, even though you would not think this by looking at the Muslim world today. The early followers of the Prophet were hungry for knowledge about Islam, and they spent time and energy compiling, verifying, and producing knowledge. This instinctive desire for knowledge is something that has been dampened in the modern world of Islam. Remember that while the Islamic community once represented knowledge, wealth, and power, today almost 70 percent of your fellow Muslims can neither read nor write. This imposes an obligation on those of us who are able to read and write. The obligation is to learn as much as we can, and spread as much knowledge as we can. This is how we can honor the memory of our Prophet as well as of those early Muslims who embarked on the search for knowledge.

There are parts of the Muslim world where girls are discouraged from having access to education. This is often presented in religious terms: girls are for the home; they will not need to learn to read or write, since their husbands will take care of them; girls should not leave the home, for fear of what strangers might do to them; girls or women should not study alongside boys because of the immorality that will ensue. All of these are reasons that are buried in the origins of traditional societies and have little or nothing to do with the basic principles of Islam. It is a reflection of a male-oriented world more than anything else. I have even heard the argument seriously made that if women are educated, they will take jobs away from deserving males. A remarkable position to take. In order to level the playing field somewhat, it needs to be said that there are also places where education itself is discouraged, as an educated population can threaten traditional systems of power and wealth. This approach applies to both male and female education. Clearly the idea of education is tied up with the fear of an empowered and capable population—male and female. These positions are unacceptable and unintelligent in the twenty-first century.

So the question of whether we are people of one book or many books is answered. We are a people of many books, of knowledge, of wisdom. But this is a title that we must earn with each generation of Muslims. We cannot rely on what was achieved by a previous generation. We need to reacquire knowledge with each generation and push its boundaries out further.

HOW WE CONSTRUCT OURSELVES
AND THE PAST

Habeebie Saif,
Every year you argue with your mother and me about your education, about your school, and about what decisions you believe you should be making without consulting us for guidance or permission. You have, like any decent child, questioned the wisdom of your parents' decisions regarding your well-being. You often feel that you could make these decisions for yourself.

What you are beginning to understand is that these decisions are all directly connected to the way in which we picture how you will be equipped to deal with the world around you when you are finally free of us. I smile as I write these words. Believe me, we want you to be free and self-reliant.

We also want you to be educated across a wide range of subjects. We want you to be alert and aware of what is going on in your immediate surroundings, as well as in the wider world. We want you to be able to face tough decisions, or difficult situations, or great challenges with confidence and a plan for getting through to the other side of these trials.

How do you think we are doing this? Well, letting a child grow like a weed is not the appropriate approach. We look at you as a child with potential, and we work with your school and with you to construct a young man who is able to realize this potential at the right time.

Saif, I think it will be interesting for you to know how I have come to think about what education I want for you and your brother, Abdullah. It is all directly related to the absence of my own father from my upbringing.

When I was younger than you are now, I had heard many wonderful things about my own father. Remember, he died when I was six years old. For years my siblings and I were told stories about him. He had been traveling from the age of twelve in the pursuit of an education. The part of the Arab world that we are from had no formal schools in the 1940s. The only education available was the local Quran school, where the children of the town would gather and memorize the Quran. Children of all ages were in the same class. There were no classes in math or literature or any of the other subjects that we take for granted today.

My father memorized the Quran and began at the age of twelve to give the sermon in the mosque on Fridays on occasion. His babysitter—an ancient woman by the time I had the opportunity to meet her—told me that he was a precocious child who spent all his available time speaking to adults and learning from their stories.

In his midteens, orphaned, he was free to pursue his desire for a formal education. He made his way to a neighboring country called Bahrain, and raced through its educational system, ranked as the top student in the country every year till he graduated from school.

My father was free as a child to do what he wanted. He pursued an education. Using an Islamic turn of phrase, he "went as far as China for knowledge."

Why am I recounting this to you, Saif? For two reasons. The first reason is that I want you to understand that even when a person is stripped of family and any income, it is possible through force of will and ingenuity for this person to forge a path through life. And by path, I mean a path of noble and worthy struggle. This your grandfather did. He had only his wits to guide him.

The second reason is that as I looked at the short life he led, I tried to imagine how he would have brought my siblings and me up. I found that no matter how much I heard about him from your grandmother or from his acquaintances, there was a tremendous void. This void was the void of not knowing him myself. The void was the emptiness of building up an impression based on other people's faulty and sometimes contradictory memories.

And then one day it dawned on me that every time I asked myself, what would my father have said?—or, what would my father have done?—I was making up the answer on the basis of what I thought was best. I was guessing what my father would have done, on the basis of a series of stories about him. I realized that in imagining what he might have done, I had a choice. I had a choice in deciding what kind of a life he would have lived.

This did not happen overnight. It took years for me to accept that there were many things I could never and can never know about your grandfather. It is painful to think that a person lives on only in the fading memories of those who knew him. And with the years, one by one his friends who could have told me more began passing away. With every passing, I could feel memories of my father being erased. And then one day I grasped the truth that I was creating an image of my father based on what I wanted him to be. And like a good son, I wanted my father to be the best father and person in the world.

This letter is partly linked to my letter to you on role models. How we model ourselves—or who we model after—is a choice. We choose how to imagine our role models, how to understand them, how to paint them, and how to bring them to life. I want you to bring the mechanism of your imagination out into the open and create yourself and the world around yourself—according to the best and highest standards.

I struggled for many years with the collective idea of my father. These were ideas that others had given me, and ideas that I myself projected onto him. So in a direct way I do not deal with his reality, but with the ideas of what he could have been, what I wanted him to be, and what he may have been had he lived longer.

I believe this was not just the moment when I began to think of the historical facts regarding my father's life and how I could construct a consistent and faithful picture of him, but also the moment when I realized that I was constructing an image that I wanted to follow. In this way, in constructing my father, I was constructing myself. In imagining my father's life and behavior, I was also imagining what kind of model I wanted to follow for myself. I remember clearly thinking of this process as bootstrapping a father role model out of my imagination and a few threadbare facts.

How does all of this connect with some of the ideas that you will face in coming to a better understanding of our Islamic faith, and the crucial task of educating ourselves in it?

Saif, my experience of trying to understand who my

father was, and how he behaved, is similar to the process that we use in understanding what happened 1,400 years ago in the cities of Mecca and Medina.

If from the distance of a few years, I have found it almost impossible to reconstruct a realistic image of my father in his social and moral complexity with any certainty, imagine how difficult it is to do the same for our Prophet and his Companions. Of course the material that has survived is voluminous. But what you need to recognize is that the power of empathy and imagination are probably more important than the disparate facts that we can collect. The facts, as they are conveyed to us, are constructions related by people who observed the Prophet. We should bear in mind that each person would come to the process of observation with his or her own interests and biases. Every person has them. Some people think that personal behavior is of utmost importance. Others think that the only thing worth remembering about another person is his or her sense of humor. Yet others will regard only occasions of philosophical brilliance worthy of memory and record. So when we look at the facts around the Prophet, we bear in mind that all of these facts are conveyed through the lens of human interest or lack thereof.

This means that our picture is clear, but necessarily incomplete. It is necessarily incomplete because there are so many things that could have been recorded with a camera, had there been cameras around. It is necessarily incomplete because the process of compiling stories and sayings started after the passing of the Prophet.

If we are to be faithful to the spirit of the Prophet, we should recognize that it takes years of pondering and digesting verses and stories and documented histories in order to begin to imagine what went on at the time of the Revelation of the Quran.

Saif, I want you to explore the ways in which the individual is constructed in the Islamic world today. Take from my experience and think about what you would do if you were to build an educational system for yourself and other Muslims. The construction and reconstruction of my identity over the years shape and inform my stance on Muslim Individualism, which I will explain in my final letter to you. This practice of constructing ourselves is what we should impart to you and your generation. Self-reflection is instrumental to understanding not just who you are but also your relevance. Building an individual identity begins by looking at yourself and discerning what characteristics are products of our family heritage and the prejudices of our wider community, as opposed to what characteristics are intrinsic to your own special and specific nature.

Remember that I realized that what I was actually

doing all those years was imagining what kind of a man my father had been and trying to model myself on this virtual father I had constructed out of the ether. He was well read. I would be also. He was moral and ethical and spiritual. I should be so too. He was kind and generous, and he sympathized with those less fortunate. So was I and so do I.

But was this truly my father? Today, I am not sure of anything. The words that are used to describe him by those who knew him are unfortunately so bereft of any real content that I know I am engaged in a fantasy construction.

I know that over many years I have constructed an idea of my father as an Arab and a Muslim and a human being. It is with a minimal number of facts and a great deal of imagination that I have built up a picture of how my father might have raised me and my siblings. What I can say with certainty is that my personal mission to build an image of my father made me appreciate not just his existence as a special human being, but also the certainty that each of us is a human being with something special to offer the world. It is my determination to fill in the gaps of his life that has made me so aware of the possibilities for each and every individual.

As I thought about who my father had been and who he might have evolved into, I began thinking very differently about what it meant to be a Muslim—but not just any Muslim. I was interested in what it took to become the best of Muslims. I wanted to know what I should read to become familiar with the references that represented the best of our literature. I wanted to know where the best congregated and what sense they held of themselves. Fairly quickly, I found that though there might be such ideas, there was no clear sense of working toward a set of goals or of working within a set of standards. If there were any clear models, they revolved around the mosques. Unfortunately, I also found that they all were characterized by an absence of rigorous thought, of depth of character, or of complex personality. I began to despair, to fight back, to run away, and to return.

In closing this letter, I want you to remember that education is more than just absorbing facts and passing exams. The education that I see for you is one that is based on an understanding that you can grow as a complex and whole individual if you recognize the role of responsible imagination in building yourself. I want you to grab hold of your imagination and force it to think through the myriad possibilities that exist for your life path. I then want you to make the choices you make, taking full and free responsibility for those choices. Why? Because that is what each of us is doing subconsciously when imagining we know things with certainty. Bring your freedom and responsibility out into the open and embrace it.

Saif, I sometimes imagine that you might one day have a sister or even two. What would be different in this letter if it were addressed to your sisters? Would I tell them that I expect something else from them and for them? In some of the more "traditional" Muslim households, girls are seen differently from boys. Is this appropriate or necessary? Is it Islamic to keep our young Muslim girls out of schools, and deprive them of an education?

In answering this question, I cannot simply look to traditional texts and strict interpretations of Islam. I also need to look at my own personal experience and see what this tells me. Dry rules in dusty books need to make sense in life, and in the light of lived experience.

My experience was to grow up in a household where my mother raised us without the presence of our father. This sets the scene for my answer to you. My mother survived, and my father did not. This was unfortunate, but there are millions of households around the Muslim world where fathers are missing, due to work, war, or death. This means that women are raising their families without the presence of their husbands.

The other factor to bear in mind is that my sister was the oldest of my siblings. She was the leader of the children—if I can describe her like this. And what a leader she was! Nothing got past her. She was sharp tongued and had a commanding presence. By far the most intelligent of the lot, she kept skipping grades due to her mental abilities. She was in control and knew what she wanted in life.

When you consider my mother's determined nature, and my sister's sparkling intelligence, and it is suggested that girls should be deprived of an education, I laugh. Every single one of us has the right to an education. And I believe every single one of us has the right to seek out the best education possible. Why would we deprive our children of great mothers and brilliant sisters? They are people in their own right, able to think and do and be. In fact, when given the chance, Muslim women far surpass the skills and education levels of Muslim men. We, as Muslim men, have no right to stand in their way.

MEN AND WOMEN

Habeebie Saif,

You have been brought up in a household where women are strong, educated, focused, and work hard. Your aunts are all highly educated and either have superb jobs or have their own businesses. They drive themselves to and from work without anyone to ask them why or where they are going.

Your mother—you know her all too well. Educated, hardworking, driven, ambitious for herself and her children. There are no weak women around you. In fact, each of them would be an excellent role model for you and your brother.

They make use of the talents that Allah has given them, and they make full use of the resources they were blessed with. What's not to admire?

All around you, when you are at home, you see women taking the lead, pushing on, striving to better themselves, and contributing to society in multiple ways. If someone suggested to you that men are by nature better and more talented than women, I know that you would likely scratch your head and wonder what they were talking about.

In reality, if you look around the world in which we live, it's the men who seem to be falling behind. I wonder why this might be the case.

After all, if you listen to any of the traditional sermons that I was accustomed to hearing as a boy your age, you would have heard that women are in some way inferior to glorious men. You would have been very pleased with the way men were described. Strong, intelligent, emotionally stable, the breadwinners of the family. Women were seen as appendages, objects to be cared for but certainly not to be taken seriously. Perhaps I am exaggerating, but this view of women in Islam certainly exists in parts of the Islamic world. It is not the only possible view of women in Islam, but it is a powerful one, supported in many cases politically, legally, and financially.

In the cases where this political, legal, and financial support for such a view exists, the description of women as passive objects to be cared for and protected from the ravages of the world becomes a self-fulfilling prophecy. It seems only logical that if you deprive someone, anyone, male or female, of the possibility of an education, of mobility, or of a sense of dignity and responsibility, then you will have participated in the act of creating a weakened human being.

Look at some of the wealthier people you and I have come across in life. Some of them have forgotten how to do the most basic things in life. If people don't come up against minimal hardship, they grow soft and weak. If a person's every wish is granted, then they never need to figure out how to do things themselves. If I give you all that you ask for, you will become spoiled. Everyone knows this when it comes to young men. Why don't we recognize that depriving women of the ability to take care of themselves is to deprive them of dignity and self-respect? In a growing number of Muslim countries, there is a recognition that everyone will benefit, both economically and socially, if women are not only permitted but actually supported in the workplace. Economic development and competition demand that all participate. And what better example than the first wife of the Prophet, Khadija, who was an independent businesswoman and the Prophet's employer?

Perhaps what we see at home is a manifestation of this rule of life. If a person who expects to be deprived of basic possibilities in life, such as education, mobility, and legal personhood, gets the opportunity to progress, they grab hold of it in a way that someone with all the privileges in life will not. This is why I think we see the women of our society progressing in education, in business, and in government so rapidly.

I am proud that your mother and your aunts are all educated and working at the top of their chosen professions. Has this stopped any of them from raising families and taking care of their husbands, as demanded by the stricter positions? Not at all. In fact, each of them is fully supported morally by their husbands.

There is something to be learned from the way we treat people. If I tie you up with rope and you are unable to walk or feed yourself, whose fault is that—yours or mine? If I educate you and treat you with respect and dignity, how are you likely to turn out?

I think you know where I am going. We cannot claim women in Islam are unable to face the big, wild world out there if it is us who have deprived them of the basic rights and skills to do so.

There is, however, another argument that some more traditional Muslim men use, and that is the argument of morality. This argument is a sensitive one. It is difficult for us to talk about it openly in our societies where relations between men and women are a taboo subject.

What it boils down to is this. If women are mobile, and independent, and working with other men, then this opens up the possibility that they will develop romantic or even sexual relations in violation of our moral code.

And the moral code that underlies this position is based on controlling women. Is this the moral code of Islam? It is one interpretation. It is not the only one.

This is a possibility. Of course it is. But it is just as much a possibility when a woman is living in a home where she is given little love and self-respect. Men who imagine that a caged bird has no desire for freedom are doing just that—imagining.

It is a fantasy to think that our Muslim women are somehow to be controlled and constrained in the very human instinct for love and affection.

I want you and me to be honest with each other. Our women need to be trusted and respected. Once we trust and respect our sisters, our mothers, our daughters, and our aunts, we might begin to see with the power of empathy how we might provide the same respect to other women in our society. If this basic respect that any human being deserves became more widespread, then perhaps we would not witness the awful cases of sexual harassment that we have heard of in the Muslim world. If we were true to our moral code of respect for the inviolability of women's dignity, then we would not violate their dignity when they are strangers to us. Women in the Muslim world are the ones who will raise us all, if given the chance.

What a comedy of errors it becomes when some of our Muslim brethren deprive their women of an education. Do they not see that these are the very women who will be raising their children? Do they not realize that an uneducated mother, wife, or daughter becomes an even greater burden because of the transmission of ignorance from one generation to the next? Do they not realize that all the women around our Prophet were strong, bold, determined women who were given the greatest respect by those around them?

Saif, I want you to see that there is nothing written in stone that puts Muslim women on a rung far below men. These are simply typical practices of patriarchal societies. Islam has no reason to disadvantage women. Every element of women's place in traditional Muslim societies, such as the veil, or a lack of mobility, or restrictions on work and education, has its roots not in Islamic doctrine, but in the fear of men that they will not be able to control their women. It is also the fear that their women will prove to be more disciplined, more focused, more hardworking, and ultimately more successful than they are. This is where I see the real problem in our Muslim societies. The fear that we men have of being overtaken by our women.

This is something that we, you and I and others, need to become aware of and work to resolve. We men are the ones who need to push aside the typical stereotypes that we have inherited and not examined. It is up to those with the power to hold people back through legal, financial, and political means to question their assumptions about their fellow human beings. And if men assume the worst of their women, perhaps it says more about men and their view of the world.

Here is a question for you that will show you the power of imagination and empathy. How would you feel if I decided to marry you off at this age and send you out into the world to find a job, and earn a living? You might think this a little unfair. You haven't finished school yet. What are the chances you might find a job? Or that this job is actually well paying, given that your education is incomplete?

You would presumably like to have some input into this decision. In fact, you would probably run off to your grandparents and tell them that I had lost my mind.

Now imagine that you have a younger sister—say thirteen years old. What if I decided one day to send her off to marry a man much older than she was? I would tell you that she did not need to finish school, as her new husband would take care of all her needs. He would clothe her and feed her. All she needed to do was take care of the house—cleaning, cooking, perhaps decorating—and have babies. I would tell you that this was the end of the road for her. She would not be a burden to me anymore.

You would probably punch me and then run off to your grandparents again. Just as you would not be prepared for a life of marriage and work while in your teens, nor would any sister of yours be ready. And believe me, both of you would feel as though you had been cheated by your parents if we really did carry out such a plan. You would likely feel that you had been deprived of a chance of living a proper life, a life of education, of decent work, of building a family at the appropriate time.

Basically you and your sister would hate me and your mother for having brought you into the world and then sent you out long before you were ready to leave home. In the same way that you would not like this for yourself, think of all the young girls who are married off far before it is appropriate—based on the argument that the Prophet married a young Aisha. Remember that possibilities for life achievement were radically different in seventh-century Arabia. In the twenty-first century, we should be shocked and angry at depriving a young girl of her chance in life. Use your sense of empathy and think about these injustices in the name of your faith.

Remember also that today Islam is a religion in transition and in conflict with itself. There are other models of how Muslim women can live and be true to our common faith. There are Muslim women who have looked into the origins of the veil and have come to the conclusion that there are no hard-and-fast rules on the veil—let alone the burqa. Many men have come to the same conclusion. Women are called on to be modest within Islam. But the veil is a pre-Islamic tradition. There are multiple ways to interpret modesty. The veil is simply one of a number of interpretations. And if there is flexibility on the question of the veil, then the burqa is simply a tradition and not religion.

FREE SPEECH AND THE SILENCE WITHIN OURSELVES

Habeebie Saif,
You will have witnessed the global debate around Islam
and the value of free speech. This reached a terrible
crescendo with the killing of the staff of *Charlie Hebdo*—
the satirical French magazine—by people claiming to be
avenging their insult of the Prophet. This incident
followed earlier incidents, such as the cartoons published
in Danish newspapers that were offensive to Islam
and Muslims. The Danish cartoons episode led to
demonstrations and riots in many Muslim cities around
the world, denouncing the insult and demanding
retribution. Another consequence of these and similar
incidents is that a number of Muslims, and Muslim
countries, have been promoting the idea of a law against
blasphemy. This campaign is taking place in European
countries as well as in the Arab world. In Islamic
countries, it is clear that insulting Islam as a faith, or

insulting the Prophet, is a serious crime. There are even those who call for the death penalty. In Pakistan, for example, politicians have been killed for suggesting that the blasphemy law should be repealed. In some Arab countries, the campaign has taken upon itself to expand the existing blasphemy laws to include insulting the Companions of the Prophet. Since the Shia are known to hold some of the Prophet's Companions in low regard, this law can be seen to be directed toward Shia sections of the community.

What are we to make of all of this? How should you approach this very broad and complex question?

I will try to answer these questions by approaching them from a different perspective. Rather than focusing on the feelings of insult and hurt that are created by the actions of others, I want to look at the place of speech in our lives.

When I was a child I remember being advised by cautious older friends to avoid controversial subjects like religion and politics. Some of my father's friends listened to my detailed questions about his strange and violent death and gently avoided answering me. Once in a while I would be pulled to one side and advised to remain quiet about things that did not matter anymore. Or I would be told bluntly to stop asking questions. I was never really sure why I should not ask the questions.

Out of some respect for my elders, as well as innate caution, I toned down my questions.

The same happened whenever I posed a question to those who purported to teach us about our religion. The questions would tumble out: How do you know Allah exists? Why should we pray? Was it not a little strange that Allah would create us in order for us to worship him? Doesn't that sound a little selfish?

Teachers or friendly adults would turn different colors, or try to laugh off the questions. These were inappropriate queries. For some, these questions were dangerous and unacceptable.

Of course, today I see these questions as the normal questions any child in the Islamic world will have, driven by the same fundamental human curiosity and need to understand that we all share.

There is nothing wrong with these questions. Perhaps there is something wrong in not allowing for them, and not attempting to make space for some answers to them.

At a certain point, I found that I knew what subjects I should not speak about. And as the years went by, I observed the empty spaces in our lives as matters of importance were glossed over, or brushed aside, with a knowing smile. These subjects covered religion, politics, sex and sexuality, mistakes and errors, anything that might make the other person "lose face." When I read the newspapers, I began to wonder whether I was living in a parallel universe. I used to wonder why we only read good news about ourselves. The real world around me abounded in errors, ethical quandaries, political catastrophes, blatant lies, and imagined glories. Perhaps not all of the time but certainly at points where I thought critical examination was vital.

I understood that there were no written rules that told me and others what we could or could not talk about. It was something in the way we had habituated ourselves. Not as members of a particular nationality, but as members of a culture and a religious machine that produced patterns of acceptable thought. This system of patterns I now see as a form of semiconscious self-censorship.

What do I mean by self-censorship? And what consequences does it have?

Self-censorship is the general feeling that something will not be accepted and is best left unsaid. It happens in many societies. Our concern here is our Muslim society, and our Muslim community.

As I grew, I would spend more time thinking about certain questions, but not asking them. I had realized that people often did not want to hear the questions. Furthermore, even if they heard the questions, they either did not want to engage with them or did not really know what to say, because they had never really made the effort to engage with the questions themselves. The end result was that the questions hovered in the back of my mind day in and day out—unanswered, unexplored. They were questions that existed only in embryonic form, because to take greater shape they needed to be uttered and accepted as legitimate.

After long periods of silence, avoiding basic, casual debate and discussion—or worse, not presenting a view, or taking a position on matters of political or social interest—I discovered that I had forgotten the matters that I had cared about in the past. It was as though the platform of my personality had been erased through the recurrence of silence. The silence that started out as the avoidance of posing questions that could be sensitive—such as the circumstances of my father's death—soon became a silence within.

The silence that develops when you are silent with yourself for too long is a haunting emptiness. This is the dumb silence that signifies an emptying out of yourself. I know that in some cultures this is a dream come true. Some people cherish the idea of quieting the mind, of avoiding the recurring thoughts and questions of modern life.

And over the years I have seen friends choose to disengage from life in the pursuit of this type of inner quiet, an inner peace.

Saif, there is another type of silence that I think of as

an Islamic silence. Perhaps it is more accurate to describe it as a religious silence, or the silence of group think. It is not intrinsic to our religion, but it manifests itself in the behavior of some of our religious leaders and self-anointed spokespeople. This silence is the kind that arises because we refuse to ask, and answer, difficult questions that arise naturally in the course of human life—no matter what ideology or religion we believe in. This is the silence that occurs when instead of answering a hard question, we decide to distract ourselves and the questioner with talk of how we should not provoke people, and that we should behave responsibly in the public sphere, or that we risk offending people if we open certain subjects.

As a Muslim, I find it unbecoming and infantilizing. Why should we Muslims be exempt from the difficult questions of life? Do we deny the reality of the questions? In some clear cases we do deny them. There are at least two examples that come to my mind. The first is the sphere of sexuality. What are we as Muslims to do with the complex idea of being born with a predisposition to homosexuality? What are we to do with the idea of not having chosen one's sexuality? We know that Islam holds a position against free choices being made, but what does Islam say in the case of someone not having chosen but having discovered their sexuality? I do not see that this discussion has begun in mainstream Islam. And yet we know that there are homosexual Muslims.

The second area in which we deny the hard questions is in the sphere of what are globally called "family values." Family values are presented as values we share with Catholics and other conservative groups in international forums. But what if "family values" hide tremendous injustice committed by patriarchal fathers against their wives and children, especially their daughters? What if once we begin to discuss and explore the reality of family values, we discover that the veneer of family values hides emotional and physical harm that ripples out silently across society through time and space?

These are two great silences that hold us back.

What happens when we impose these silences upon ourselves and others? What happens when we reject the articulation of our lives through publicly uttered statements? What happens when we look around ourselves and begin to realize that our silence has led to an absence of ideas, a dampened vitality, a floating thoughtlessness, a silence of the mind?

I can tell you from my experiences that one of the repercussions is that one's thoughtlessness is quietly replaced by the convictions of others.

I was fourteen when I took my mother's advice regarding silence very seriously. I had just emerged from a period of intense piety and devotion, and what I call religious silence, during which I deserted old friends because they were either not Muslim or insufficiently religious. But I discovered that the effect of my religious silence was that it crippled me. I panicked and decided that I needed to stop this paralysis of thought. I had no opinions anymore. Or at least no opinions that I would really stand up for. I was continually defending myself against questions with the reply: I don't know, or I am not sure. I had disengaged myself from thinking about matters for long enough that I had no means by which to reengage. I wanted to participate. I wanted to argue and discuss and be passionate about things. Instead I sat on the sidelines of the debates and verbal battles that took place around me.

As I left the religious silence that I had imposed upon myself in my attempt to be the so-called good Muslim, I discovered there was the silence of not having any certainties to work with or from.

I had been so convinced in my piety and devotion, and now my simple and straightforward convictions had been shaken—by the complexity of the questions that kept surging into my conscious mind. What could I be certain about now? And if I could not be certain about anything, what could I talk about?

I found that I no longer had a starting point. This is an exceptionally dangerous position to be in, both emotionally and intellectually. It is at this point that a person will begin grasping at any semblance of certainty, if only to participate in life with others.

Beware of these silences. If you are going to live in the real world, the world of anger, violence, love and passion, responsibility, and continuity, then silence is not the path I recommend. You need to put yourself in the world, and in the way of the world. You need to stand in the face of the elements and watch the world carve away at your young self. With time, and with purposeful experience, you will discover the elements of your deeper self that you can call your own. By purposeful experience, I mean going out and placing yourself in positions where you are compelled by circumstances to take responsibility. Climb a mountain. Volunteer with children in a poverty-stricken country. Help a friend out of trouble. Defend someone less privileged than yourself. Teach someone how to read and write. Speak in public and hear what people think of you. You will refine your understanding of yourself in the same way that a sculptor releases a figure from a block of marble.

Speaking out loud in public with people is a vital part of this process of self-discovery. And self-discovery is part of the process of assuming responsibility as an individual in the world. It is through speech that we identify ourselves and we dialogue with others. There is no community without some form of speech. The more wide-ranging and complex the speech, the greater service we will be to each other and to ourselves. And it is through the refined use of speech that we take moral responsibility for the world around us.

Saif, I believe each of us, as an individual, has an obligation to speak and to do so freely. I also believe that we have an obligation to speak openly and freely as Arabs in the Arabic language with one another, and with those outside our linguistic world, in order to feel the rub of strange ideas, revealing metaphors, and perplexing histories. And finally, I believe that we as Muslims have an obligation to talk openly and freely with one another, as well as with those of other faiths, in order to enrich our understanding of ourselves and others.

A CLOSER LOOK AT A
MORAL CONUNDRUM

Habeebie Saif,

You will have come across a lot of Muslims who shake
their heads at the state of the Muslim world and mutter
the words "If only people were proper Muslims, then
none of this would be happening." I have heard this
type of utterance so many times over the course of my
life. It is used when criticizing corruption in Muslim
countries, or pointing out the spread of "moral"
corruption. It is also used by those who promote various
forms of Islamic rule. The most famous example of this
was the slogan "Islam Is the Solution," which was used
by the Muslim Brotherhood political-religious party in
Egypt throughout its long history there.

I always used to wonder what the problem was if
Islam was the solution. But, of course, this is precisely
the point they were making. They were saying that any
problem that we face in life, from personal to political,

from moral to economic, is solvable by being better Muslims.

The Egyptian Muslim Brotherhood—a religious political party founded in 1928—took this approach to the extreme, and did not even really spend much time thinking about how they would use political power, or even what political power was for. This is perhaps the reason why they then lost power in Egypt almost as quickly as they got hold of it in 2012.

Let's be honest. The slogan was a brilliant one. Lots of people believed in it. Lots of people still believe in it. When I was younger I believed in it wholeheartedly. But something in me changed over the years. I will explain why it is possible to be a devout and pious Muslim without needing to believe that Islam Is the Solution in every case.

One of the most extreme examples of the idea that Islam Is the Solution can be found in the appearance of ISIS in 2014 in Syria and Iraq. Deep down inside, the argument that is being made is that all the most glorious periods in Islamic history—the conquests, the empires, the intellectual achievement, the wealth—occurred under what seems to have been Islamic rule. Therefore, if we want to acquire this past glory in the modern era, we need to impose a system of Islamic rule that covers every aspect of life. Why would this be logical? If a little Islam is good, then more Islam is better. And if more

Islam is better, then complete Islam must be best. Who in today's Muslim world would be prepared to argue with this position?

Let's look at ISIS then and see what problems this approach might bring and what solutions it might provide. ISIS is an example of uncontrolled, unbridled enthusiasm for the all-encompassing religious-state position. In the Arab and Islamic worlds, the overall narratives of ISIS can seem correct—even if the extremes of violence and aggression can seem out of place.

How might it be seen as correct? Well, because the model that ISIS proposes is something that made sense in the Islamic world—once upon a time. ISIS is very clever in appealing to old models that are buried in dusty histories that we can neither confirm nor deny with any ease. Certainly not with any ease in traditional Muslim societies, where we all want to be a little more successful globally than we currently are. Therefore their easy and straightforward approach to an all-encompassing Muslim way of life—politically, socially, economically, and morally—appeals to certain groups.

For this reason, different authoritative Islamic figures and groups have declined to condemn ISIS on the basis that ISIS is Muslim but acting incorrectly on some issues. This is truly unfortunate but in accordance with a set of relatively widespread narratives of Islam, which is worrying. If we take ISIS to be representative of a possible design solution, then we need—as Muslims—to recognize which problems it solves and which problems it creates.

ISIS is an extension of the argument—Islam Is the Solution—often heard by those despairing of poor government services or corruption in pre-2011 Arab countries. This position is similar to the one that proposes vaguely that sharia—or traditional Islamic law as defined by centuries of Islamic scholarship—be imposed as the law of the land.

What is really being proposed is that if we declare that we are acting in Allah's name, and if we impose the laws of Islam, and if we ensure the correct mental state of the Muslim population living in this chosen territory, then Allah will intervene to solve the problems of the modern Arab and Islamic worlds—illiteracy, poverty, hunger, suffering, and weakness.

The brilliance of this model—and it is a model that is openly proposed by the Muslim Brotherhood—is that any failure can be attributed to the lack of faith and piety of the population. That's it. Nothing else is required. The response to failure is to look into ourselves and condemn ourselves for not being pious enough.

This is a model that is not unique to Islam, and is not unique to the era of the Muslim Brotherhood or of ISIS. It is an ancient model built on the expectation that the divine intervenes to save those who are worthy of being saved. This model is also underpinned by the conflation of religion with life. This is the direct result of the Islamist conflation of religion and existence.

When religion is life, there is no escaping the divine's wrath or reward.

The following illustration is a famous account of the Prophet Mohammed who happened upon some people who were busy conducting pollination experiments on date crops. To these individuals he said, "If you would not do this, then it would still come out right." They followed the Prophet's advice and stopped their experimentation. The resulting date crop was of very poor quality.

When he saw them again, he inquired about the failure of their work. "What is with your date palms?" he asked. They explained to the Prophet that they had stopped trying their method of pollination after receiving his advice. In return he said, "You know best the affairs of your worldly life."

When the divine stands apart from his creation, and religion is conjoint with, but not identical to, life, we open up to the possibility of responsibility. It is from within this position that we can design a different political system that gives religion its sphere of activity that will separate out those areas in which all humankind is expected to intervene by using his or her mind and his or her physical energy. Very simply put, there is within the basic tradition of Islam the concept that the divine helps he who helps himself.

If there is a battle of ideas within Islam, then this is the key battle. It is the battle for taking responsibility directly for the problems we complain about. It is a battle less of ideas than it is a battle of coherent ideas. As we discuss ideas, it is also vital that we shout out loudly to each other what the consequences of our beliefs are. If the consequences of our beliefs are that we end up in a failed state with our throats being cut by the self-appointed who deem themselves more pious than the rest of us, then we need to know about it. Most Muslims, I suspect, would reject this power-crazed bloodshed if they could. Thus, consequences and implications are vitally important in mapping out new possibilities for the Muslim world. It is our coherence of vision and the clarity of our analysis that will be vital to the future of the Muslim world. We need to understand that piety will take us far, but relying entirely on Allah to provide for us, to solve our problems, to feed and educate and clothe our children, is to take Allah for granted. The only way we can raise the status of the

Muslim world is by doing what all other peoples in the world do: educate ourselves, work hard, and find the answers to life's difficult questions.

Islam Is the Answer, because Islam calls upon us to take responsibility for our own lives.

THE MUSLIM INDIVIDUAL

Habeebie Saif,
In all the letters I have written to you I touch on the
idea of responsibility and choice. Sometimes I am overt
about it, and sometimes I leave these ideas in the
background. Responsibility for our actions and choosing
which actions to undertake are central to the idea of
being an individual. Of course, community is important.
Family, clan, and tribe all play their roles in helping us
to locate ourselves in the world. But I do not want you
to hide behind the achievements or positions of others.
I want you to be able to stand on your own as an
individual and be able to state clearly what you believe,
what you choose to do with your life, and what actions
you will take in the future. I want you and your
generation to be able to take a step back from all the
traditions, customs, rites, and rituals you are told are cast
in stone, and I want you to consider what you might

think is reasonable. What do you think of all of these injunctions and commands? Does any of it make sense? If it does not, then what does? It is up to you to decide.

More broadly, I believe we are in need of a vision of an improved Muslim individual and an improved Muslim world. Unfortunately, as far as I can tell, the individual today has no place in the calculations of the major groupings of the Muslim world—except perhaps as cannon fodder in the various jihadist campaigns called for by some of our more extreme religious leaders.

Tell me, Saif, when have you ever heard of the Muslim individual, or of Muslim Individualism? You hear of the Arab Nation, the Islamic Ummah, the Rightly Guided People, the Arab Street, but do you ever hear of the Muslim individual as a separate entity, a living being, a person with a character and a personality that is separate and distinct from those around him or her?

The Islamic Ummah—or community—is a term used by the Prophet Mohammed for the tribal communities of the early Islamic period that were ultimately unified by the religion. The Prophet spoke about the Ummah, or the Muslim community. This makes sense. He had built a sufficiently large group of followers that at some stage it became big enough to be called a community. As the idea of the community developed, something changed, and almost without noticing, we Muslims began to talk about the Ummah as something separate from ourselves as Muslims—as though there was a sense in which the community was more important than the members that made it up. In today's world the idea of the Ummah has become very powerful. So powerful that we often aren't even aware that there are choices that have been made for us by the leading spokesmen of Islam. The idea of the Ummah in today's world is highly politicized and casually mixes religion with the state. That means it mixes your private devotion with political power—the power to change people's lives, and the power to wage war.

Saif, I will give you an example of how this idea of the Ummah has become very powerful, and how certain political groups have tried to use it.

The Muslim Brotherhood has propagated the idea of the Ummah in the modern world. Like many other Islamist organizations, it makes the claim that it speaks on behalf of the Muslim Ummah. It makes the claim that it is able to identify the interests of the Muslim Ummah, and that it can determine what sacrifices normal individual Muslims should be making to increase the power and success of the Muslim Ummah.

ISIS makes similar claims about defending Islam and the Muslim Ummah. It is as though the global Muslim community has been repeatedly hijacked.

Self-appointed people speak in the name of the Muslim community without ever asking us what we think of their representation.

These same people then set up an opposition between the Islamic world and the Western world, between Islam and capitalism, between Islam and imperialism. In this manner, they quickly move to oppose Islamization to "Westernization." There is an ideological battle that has been raging in the Arab and Muslim worlds for more than a century around the ideas of the self versus the group, of tradition and modernity, and of religion and existence. These battles are all transformed into a larger battle between Islam and the West. You need to be aware of this battle and you need to think about whether it is really necessary.

This mechanism of a grand opposition between Islam and the West is presented as the best way to protect the Ummah's identity and secure the religion.

In the notional battle between Islamism and Westernization, the individual's voice comes second to the group's voice. It must mean something that it even sounds odd to speak of the Muslim individual. We have been trained over the years to put community ahead of any individuality. The Muslim individual—it sounds so solitary, so desperately unnatural. It is almost as though it is absent as a mental category in our Muslim worldview. Perhaps I am exaggerating, but these are the feelings I get when I say the words to myself.

But what if I am not exaggerating? I think that we in the Muslim world could solve a lot of our problems and resolve many of our recurring dilemmas if we took hold of what I believe to be this missing piece in our worldview. What if creating a dialogue and a public debate about what it means to be an individual in the Muslim world will allow us to create some mental, and perhaps social and political, space for a regeneration of Muslim societies? What if by talking about the possibility of the Muslim individual we could begin to talk about personal responsibility, and ethical choices, and the respect and dignity that attaches to the person rather than to the family, the tribe, the sect, or the religious affiliation?

What if we stop, for a moment, insisting on our group responsibilities to the mosque, the sect, or the Islamic Ummah? Perhaps we could start afresh by reframing our responsibilities to ourselves, and to others as well. Rather than asking one another about family name and bloodlines and religious sect, we might each determine to respect the individual before us no matter what background they have. And at a more mundane, prosaic level, what if speaking about the Muslim individual gives us a better insight into what is wrong with our education system and our job market and our health systems? And, of course, our political systems.

It has become clearer to me over the years since 9/11 that even if I am incorrect in diagnosing the absence of the Muslim individual from our way of looking at the world, there is at least much merit in bringing the Muslim individual to the fore in terms of the way we look at the Muslim world. Perhaps it is time to really dig deep into our culture and our politics and think about why the Muslim individual might be the best starting point for a discussion that can then take us to questions of politics, the economy, safety and security, and global peace.

It is when you and your generation start looking at one another and yourselves as individuals that you may begin to build better societies. It is when you look at each other as individuals that you will begin to memorialize the insane number of people killed in the Arab and Muslim world through civil wars and suicide bombings. It is when you and your generation memorialize, not the overall number, but the individual names and photos and life stories of each victim of our own follies that you will begin on the path to building a society that can move forward beyond the impotence and death and destruction that we are all too familiar with. This is not the feared deification of the dead, but rather a recognition of our responsibility to preserve their honor and dignity in life and in death.

There is a powerful answer or response to these very heavy demands, which is that you and your generation can each be a True Muslim in your own way. Your essence is defined by the choices you make and the actions you take.

This is where you need to take hold of your fate, to take hold of your lives, and to begin to craft yourselves step by step.

Saif, I really believe that the idea of the Muslim individual is the simplest and most effective unit for the regeneration of the Muslim world. There is no need for us to build bombs and regiments and religious cults that promise a return to a glorious past in order to build a glorious future. Our personal, individual interests may not align with those of the patriarch, the family, the tribe, the community, or the state. But the expression of each Muslim's individuality will lead to a rebalancing of our society in favor of more compassion, more understanding, and more empathy.

If you begin to accept the individual diversity of your fellow Muslims, you are likely to do the same for those of other faiths as well. Neither as Muslims nor as Arabs are we the only people in the world. We can and should live in harmony with other people in a crowded world. As long as we do not recognize the individual within our societies, we will not be able to live with humanity outside of our faith.

In ending these letters to you, Saif, I want you to promise yourself that you will always maintain your dignity, your individuality, and your independence of mind. If you can do this, you will be likelier to see life for what it is and what it can be. You will be the decider of your own path. You should also insist on discerning the dignity, individuality, and independence of mind in others. By presuming others are similarly endowed, you will create the space for them to rise to the challenge, to express themselves, and to live up to our highest standards. Now go and write your own letters.

ACKNOWLEDGMENTS

There are many people who helped me in writing this book. Most of them do not even know it. I would like to thank my wife and children for inspiring me daily and for keeping my feet on the ground. I thank Andy Eley, Andy Brown, Darren Mortimer, and David Ross as well as the infamous Volodya for listening to me when they did not need to do so. Many thanks to Emily Goodrich, who helped me immensely when I was lost in pages of text. And many thanks also to Karen Wolny for being such a great and encouraging editor. I am also most grateful to Macmillan and Picador, as well as Stefan von Holtzbrinck for having faith in what I have to say. And finally, I thank Matt of the snowy mountain for his genius in lateral thinking.